# The Bridge of Sino-Philippines Friendship

Marking the 600th Anniversary of the Visit to China by the Sultans of Sulu

王守栋 著

胡延峰 译

纪念苏禄王访华六百周年

奎章

Written by Wang Shoudong
Translated by Hu Yanfeng

GUANGXI NORMAL UNIVERSITY PRESS
广西师范大学出版社
·桂林·

# Preface I

"The Bridge of Sino-Philippines Friendship, Marking the 600th Anniversary of the Visit to China by the Sultans of Sulu" is a welcome addition to materials published on the journey of Sultan Paduka Batara to China in 1417. This book offers the perspectives of Chinese scholars and their interpretation of the significance of this voyage on Philippines-China relations.

According to accounts, Sultan Paduka Batara, together with other local chieftains and their families sailed from the Philippines to China in 1417 for an audience with the Yongle Emperor. The emperor accorded the mission with a royal reception and provided them with gifts, food and maintenance. On the return voyage a month later, the Sultan fell ill and died in Dezhou. Chinese authorities built a tomb monument in his honor, which is said to be one of the very few dedicated to a foreign dignitary on Chinese soil.

The Sultan's expedition to China is a testament to the long-standing ties between the Filipino and Chinese peoples. Hundreds of years before the official establishment of diplomatic relations in 1975, the peoples of our two countries have been engaging with one another through trade and other exchanges.

Thus, I hope this book and other similar publications will kindly interest and encourage more research on this important historical exchange between the Philippines and China.

JOSE SANTIAGO L. STA. ROMANA
Ambassdor of the Philippines to China

Beijing, 21 June 2018

# 序 一

　　《奎章——纪念苏禄王访华六百周年》是记录苏禄王 1417 年来华访问的珍贵资料。这本书以中国学者的历史考证为视角，阐明了此次访华对菲中关系的重大意义。

　　据记载，1417 年，苏禄东王巴都葛叭哈剌与西王、峒王等当地首领携同家眷，从菲律宾远渡重洋前往中国，得到了明朝永乐皇帝的隆重接待。永乐皇帝为此举办了盛大的宴会，并赠与苏禄王一行真金白银、绫罗绸缎等丰厚的礼品。在一个月后的返程中，苏禄东王巴都葛叭哈剌不幸病逝于山东德州。中国政府为表纪念，为他在德州修建了一座陵墓，这是在中国境内仅有的几座外国君主陵墓之一。

　　苏禄王访华之旅展现出菲律宾和中国人民之间的友谊源远流长。在 1975 年中菲两国正式建交前的数百年里，两国人民便一直通过贸易和其他交往方式建立紧密联系。

　　因此，我希望这本书和其他类似的出版物能引起人们的兴趣，并鼓励人们对菲律宾和中国之间这一重要的历史交流进行更多的研究。

琼斯·圣地亚哥·罗马纳

（菲律宾驻华大使）

2018 年 6 月 21 日于北京

# Preface II

Assalamualaikum! Greetings of Peace!

A strong history can build a strong nation. An echo of wisdom came from the late Professor Yap that is proven true by China. Only in China that our great ancestor Sultan Paduka Batara, then referred to as the "East King" whose roots originated from Sulu is being revered, honored and remembered.

This book, "The Bridge of Sino-Philippines Friendship, Marking the 600th Anniversary of the Visit to China by the Sultans of Sulu" is a testimony of its existence and historical journey. It also describes in detail the series of events that happened over 600 years ago. Chinese historians documented that he ruled and reigned in Sulu, pioneered maritime travel, sea expedition and established diplomatic relations in China. Sultan Batara was not only an Eastern king to the emperor, but was embraced as a brother. This is evidenced by his regal memorial that still stands today 600 years later.

The greatest truth is that we share the same history. I am forever thankful to the nobility of the leaders of China from the reign of Emperor Yong Le in 1417 down to every generation then on, they have recognized, honored and paid tribute to our rich history and culture up to this day. As the daughter of Jamalul Kiram III and the descendant of the Sultan of Sulu, allow me to use this opportunity to rekindle the ties set forth by our forefathers as a unifying experience for all of us.

I salute and congratulate Prof. Wang and Guangxi Normal University Press for writing this book. Let us continue and celebrate history today as we start and declare yet another 600 years of enduring friendship of Philippines and China beyond borders. God bless Philippines and China.

Princess Jacel H. Kiram

July 2018

# 序 二

安赛俩目阿来库姆！我谨向读者朋友们致以和平的问候！

伟大的历史可以造就一个伟大的国家。已故叶教授的这句至理名言在中国得到了印证。只有在中国，我们伟大的祖先巴都葛叭哈剌——苏禄国的东王，才会受到如此的尊崇与爱戴，并为众人所铭记。

《奎章——纪念苏禄王访华六百周年》记录了这次历史性的远航。书中详细描述了600多年前发生的一系列事件。据中国史学家考证，巴都葛叭哈剌当时统治着苏禄国，在他的引领下，苏禄国开创性地搭建起了海上航行、探险之路，并与中国建立了外交关系。对于中国明朝的永乐皇帝而言，苏禄王巴都葛叭哈剌不仅仅是东王，更如同兄弟。这般情义，毋庸置疑。为他而建的纪念碑，在600年后的今天仍然矗立，便是最好的见证。

而更为重要的是，我们两国共同参与了这一段历史，成就了一段佳话。我永远铭记并感恩1417年时的中国永乐皇帝以及其后的中国政府，时至今日，他们对我国丰富的历史和文化给予了承认、理解和尊重。作为苏禄王的后裔，贾马鲁尔·基拉姆三世的女儿，请允许我借用这个宝贵的机会将前辈为构建两国关系而系下的结再次牢牢系紧，以永续双方的团结与友谊。

《奎章——纪念苏禄王访华六百周年》已出版，在此，我祝贺王守栋教授和广西师范大学出版社，并致以崇高的敬意。让我们缅怀这段历史，并以此为基础，进一步谱写菲律宾与中国友谊的新篇章，展望下一个辉煌的600年。衷心祝愿菲中两国越来越好。

杰赛尔·基拉姆公主

2018 年 7 月

# Brief

In the 15<sup>th</sup> year of the reign of Emperor Yongle Reign during the Ming Dynasty (1417 A.D.), a large goodwill mission with hundreds of members was led by Paduka Pahala, Mahala Chigemading and Baduge Balabo. They ploughed through the billowy west Pacific Ocean to China to pay tribute to the Ming Dynasty Emperor, which started a friendly journey recorded in history forever. They traveled along the route then known as the East Ocean Run. It was one important part of the old Maritime Silk Road, linking China with Southeast Asia and African states. This sea route dated back from the Qin-Han Dynasties and continued to flourish in the Tang Dynasty. It was in the Ming Dynasty during the reign of Emperor Yongle that it became the busiest sea route across Europe, Asia and Africa, linking two oceans.

As early as the days of the Qin-Han Dynasties, our Chinese ancestors paved and opened the sea route between China and Southeast Asia. Chinese trade ships were able to reach the Persian Gulf and the eastern coast of Africa during the periods of Sui to the Tang Dynasty. It was then that China began the frequent communication with the island states of the Philippines. Maritime Silk Road developed further in the Song Dynasty, and therefore many countries and regions such as Korea, Japan, Southeast Asia and Arab states all flocked to trade with China. The Chinese grand navigation times reached the peak and Zheng He's Voyages were a great feat in the world's navigation history, which marked the heyday of the Maritime Silk Road.

Before the Sulu mission arrived in China, Zheng He with his great members sailed westward all the way via Southeast Asia to bring goodwill and peaceful diplomatic relations abroad. This attracted the neighboring states along the Maritime Silk Road as they came together. Encouraged by this trend, Sultans of Sulu took great troubles on the sea in arriving to China. They admired China as they witnessed the brilliant culture and prosperity of the Chinese people. Unfortunately, Paduka Pahala died of a disease on his way back and was buried in Dezhou City. Dezhou is a very important port along the Grand Canal, which became an eternal witness of the Sino-Philippine Friendship.

Hundreds of years later, we have stepped into the 21$^{st}$ century. As the society develops with high speed, it is faced with a new plight. We have walked into a new era of great development, great change and great adjustment. The whole world has been searching for the new engine for economic growth, the new way for trade cooperation and the new common bond for mutual dialogue. Nowadays, all eyes are focused on the Orient, on China.

In response to the consensus and the demand for construction of the human community with the common destiny, this Maritime Silk Road opened by our ancestors is now taking on the new vitality and becoming the new route for the international cooperation, mutual learning and mutual benefit. Sulu Sultans' visit to China 600 years ago established a friendly bridge for two nations and has set a good example for the 21$^{st}$ century Maritime Silk Road. This is a peaceful, booming, open, innovative and civilized road. It is noteworthy to mention that in Dezhou, where Sulu Sultan Paduka Pahala was laid to rest, his descendants were integrated into the native community. They formed two big families, the An and Wen Clans. To date, they are Chinese citizens with Sulu genes in their blood. This book represents that period of our common history.

Chairman Xi Jinping said that "this pioneering undertakings were crowned with eternal glory that the pioneers depended on camels and goodwill, rather than the war horses and spears, on the treasure ships and friendship, rather than battle ships and batteries." At present, 600 years after Sulu Sultans' visit to China, this sea route backed with a 2,000 year old history takes on with a new vitality and bears a new historical mission at the same time. It is rooted in the thick historical soil that faces the expanse of the continents of Asia, Europe and Africa. It displays openness and inclusiveness with the vastness of the Pacific and Indian Oceans. When big vessels are ready to set sail with whistle out of the busy ports, they have carried the deep friendship between responsible great powers and foreign countries. This lead to a common expectation of the countries along the 21$^{st}$ Century Maritime Silk Road.

# 自序

　　1417 年，烟波浩渺、水天一色的西太平洋上，古苏禄国的东国首领巴都葛叭答剌、西国首领麻哈剌叱葛剌麻丁、峒国首领叭都葛巴剌卜一行数百人，沿着"东洋航线"航行，开启了永载史册的一次友谊之旅。此行的目的地，是正处"永乐盛世"的中国大明。苏禄王此次访华经行的"东洋航线"，正是古代中国和南洋、欧非诸国往来交通的"海上丝绸之路"的重要部分。这条"海上丝绸之路"，溯源秦汉，经历唐宋的繁华，直至永乐盛世的熙攘，成为跨越欧亚非、连接两大洋的重要商路，也是古代中国和域内外友邦互通有无、和平交往的重要纽带。

　　早在秦汉时期，各国先民就在广袤的中华大地和南洋诸国之间，擘画出了清晰的海上航线。沿着隋唐时期的"广州通海夷道"，中国的商船可以顺利到达波斯湾和非洲东海岸。也正是从这时开始，中国与菲律宾群岛诸多古国有了频繁的交往。有宋一代，海上丝路进一步发展，从东北亚的朝鲜、日本，到南洋诸国、阿拉伯世界，都争相与中国发展海外贸易。迄于明代，中国的大航海时代达到高峰，大航海家郑和的七下西洋，标志着海上丝路发展到了极盛时期。

　　在苏禄王的盛大访华团到达中国之前，郑和就已带着庞大的使团，多次经由南洋诸国一路西行，宣扬中华民族协和万邦、向往和平的美好愿望，使"海上丝绸之路"沿线国家纷纷慕义而来。顺应彼时海上交往空前繁盛的潮流，苏禄王一行跨越万里海波，来到他们倾慕已久的中国，目睹了东方礼仪之邦博大精深的文化和繁荣富庶的经济。东王巴都葛叭答剌在归途中不幸染疾，长眠在漕运要冲——中国德州，为中菲友好交往留下了永恒的见证。

　　风云变幻，烟波沉寂。500 多年后的 21 世纪，人类社会在高速前进的同时，也面临着新的困境，进入了大发展、大变革、大调整的时代。在寻求世界经济增长的新动力、国际贸易合作的新通道、各国人民互通的新纽带时，人们把目光聚焦到了东方，聚焦到了中国。

而由诸多先行者扬帆远航、劈波斩浪开辟出的连接东西方的"海上丝绸之路"，应全球人类命运共同体建设的共识和需要，重新焕发出生机和活力，成为域内外国家合力谋求和平合作、互学互鉴、互利共赢的新航道。而苏禄王访华在开拓中菲友好交往中彰显的求索之志、架起的友谊桥梁、传达的和平善意，无疑成为将这条"21世纪海上丝绸之路"建设成"和平之路""繁荣之路""开放之路""创新之路""文明之路"的重要启迪和示范力量。更为难能可贵的是，在当年苏禄王长眠的中国德州，由留华守墓的苏禄王后人不断绵延生息而形成的安温家族，已经世代定居中国，融入中华民族大家庭。他们身上的苏禄王族基因，也似一条永恒的纽带，让跨越时空的中菲两国心灵相通、命运相融。而《奎章——纪念苏禄王访华六百周年》为我们呈现的，正是以中菲两国为代表的海上丝路域内外国家从初遇到相知的赤诚以待、从筚路蓝缕到互利共荣的同心同向、从共度时艰到共创未来的命运与共。

正如习近平总书记所说："这些开拓事业之所以名垂青史，是因为使用的不是战马和长矛，而是驼队和善意；依靠的不是坚船和利炮，而是宝船和友谊。"在苏禄王访华600年后的今天，这条绵延了2000多年的海上航道，又禀赋了新的生命，承载了新的使命。它根植于厚重的历史土壤，面向幅员广袤的亚欧非大陆，用太平洋和印度洋的浩瀚展示着自己开放包容的襟怀。当一个个繁忙港口中的大船鸣笛起航时，浪花之上，托起的将是中国作为负责任大国与域内外国家的深厚友谊，是"21世纪海上丝绸之路"沿线国家对繁荣与和平的共同期许。

# 目 录
## CONTENTS

讲述中菲历史上最美好的往事……

# Chapter I
# Historical Origin of Sino–Philippines Relations before the Ming Dynasty

More than 2,000 years ago, Zhang Qian, an envoy of the Western Han Dynasty, was sent to visit the Western Regions. He completed the globally watched diplomatic journey and pioneered the Land Silk Road as he opened the door of communications between the west and the east. At the same time, a Maritime Silk Road linking China with Southeast Asia and the Indian Ocean gradually came into existence. From then on, China began to move towards the sea and embarked towards the world. The Philippine Islands, which is separated from China by waters, also began its journey to China from a vision via this Maritime Silk Road. The friendly relationship lasting more than one thousand years between the countries drew the curtain.

# 积厚流光

## ——明代以前中菲关系的历史渊源

第 一 章

两千多年前，张骞出使西域，完成了举世瞩目的"凿空之旅"，开辟了陆上丝绸之路，打开了中西交流的大门。与此同时，汉武帝派出的使团与商船从中国东南部的海港扬帆起航，一条连接中国—东南亚—印度洋的海上丝绸之路逐步形成。从此，中国走向了大洋，走向了世界。而与中国一水之隔的邻邦——菲律宾，同样循着这条海上通道，走进了中国，由此开启了中菲两国长达千年的友好往来。

# *Pioneering the Ancient Maritime Silk Road*

## 走向大洋——古代海上丝绸之路的开辟

The ancient China originates from the Yellow River, nearly secluded from the outside world. Its east and south is the most unmanageable Pacific, its west is the precipitous Tibetan Plateau, its northwest is bounded by the continuous desert, and its north is the unbroken Gobi. In spite of the such abominable surroundings, the Chinese were not afraid of the dangers and difficulties to build the wide relations with the outside world.

发祥于黄河流域的古代中国，与外部世界是相对隔绝的。她的东面和南面是难以征服的地球第一大洋——太平洋，西南是世界上最高最险峻的青藏高原，西北是茫茫无际的万里黄沙，北面是难以逾越的戈壁荒原。尽管处于这样的地理环境，中国人依然努力冲破高山大海的险阻，渴望与外部世界建立广泛的联系。

"伏羲氏刳木为舟，剡木为楫。舟楫之利，以济不通，致远以利天下。"（《易经·系辞下》）舟的出现，扩大了人类的活动范围，可以让人不受约束地远离陆地海岸。早在远古时代，中国沿海一带的先民就开始了原始的航海活动。在20世纪70年代发掘的浙江余姚河姆渡遗址中，出土了八支罕见的木桨，还采集到一件完整的舟形陶器。经碳-14测年法测定，这只陶舟为距今7000年的物品。此外，在遗址中还发现大量鲸鱼、鲨鱼等大型海洋动物的骨头。由

**Wood Pulp on the Special Stamp: Hemudu Ruins**
**《河姆渡遗址》特种邮票**

1996年5月12日，中华人民共和国邮电部发行了一套《河姆渡遗址》特种邮票，其中，《划桨行舟》主图即选用了出土的两支木桨（距今7000—6500年）。河姆渡文化不仅代表了长江流域的文化起源，也透露出了华夏大地海洋文明的曙光

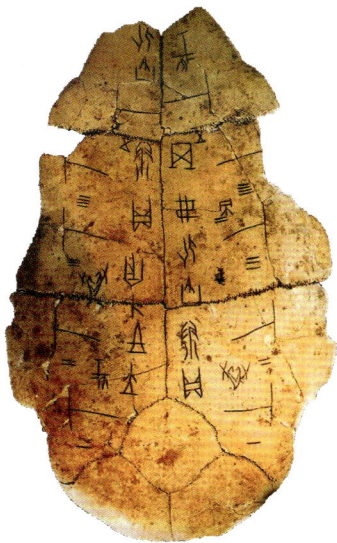

**Oracle Bone with Inscriptions**
**刻着卜辞的甲骨**

1936年，在河南安阳殷墟小屯村北YH127坑出土的属于
商朝武丁时期（公元前1250年—前1192年）的卜甲中，
有一版特大的龟腹甲，经专家鉴定，认为它是产于马来
半岛的陆龟。在英国剑桥大学收藏的《金璋所藏甲骨卜
辞》中，第五五四版龟甲残片与众不同。经鉴定，这是
棕褐大龟的腹甲。这种大龟分布于缅甸至印度尼西亚一
带。这表明，殷商时期，中国与东南亚地区已经存在文
化上的接触（参见李喜所主编《五千年中外文化交流史》，
世界知识出版社2002年版，第33页）

此可以推断，早在新石器时代，居住在东南沿海之滨的中
国先民就广泛使用独木舟，并以其非凡的勇气与智慧开始
了对海洋的探索。

"乙亥卜，行贞，王其□舟于河，亡灾。"（《殷墟书
契前编》）这段甲骨上的卜辞记载了商王在河中泛舟、平
安无事的状况。记载着这些卜辞的甲骨，除了来自黄土高
原的牛骨，更多的则是产自南方深海的龟甲。而卜辞中出
现的晦（海）、涛、龟、鱼等与大海有关的文字，则透出
浓浓的海洋气息。

秦汉时期，中国形成"大一统"的局面，并加大了对
外交往的力度，面向蔚蓝色的海洋，拓展海上贸易。当时
中国航海技术取得进步，造船业、航海业获得发展，在东
部和东南沿海的东莱郡（今山东烟台和威海一带）、会稽
郡（今江苏南部，浙江、福建东部地区）、南海郡（今广
东珠江三角洲及其以东地区）等地，有专门的造船基地。

西汉武帝时期，国力强盛，在向西开辟陆上丝绸之路
的同时，积极通过海路向外拓展，派遣使节、商船出使南

As early as the ancient times, the Chinese people living in the southeast coast began to use the canoe to explore the oceans with incomparable courage and wisdom. In the Shang Dynasty, turtle shells from south sea were used as the oracle bones for divination as recorded in history, aside from the ox bones from Loess Plateau. Some characters from the oracle inscriptions such as sea, wave, turtle and fish showed the intensive maritime features.

In the period of the Qin and Han Dynasty, our country established a unified feudal regime and strengthened the relationship with the outside world to explore maritime trades.

**Ship Building Ruins of Qin Dynasty**
**秦代造船遗址**

据《史记》记载，秦始皇平定岭南时，当时驻扎在番禺（今广州）的一支秦军，专门建造大量的船只，供平定瓯越所需。1974年，考古工作者在广州发现秦代造船工厂遗址

The sites of the imperial palace of Nanyue State and the shipyard of the Qin-Han Period found in Guangzhou seemed to be a historical witness that the ancient Chinese people sailed along the Maritime Silk Road. According to the description in Geography Chronicles, from History of the Former Han Dynasty, we can clearly see a sea route between the vast expanse of China and Southeast Asia. At that time, the Chinese merchant ships had

洋、西洋诸国，建立、发展与海外诸国的政治、经济和文化交流。公元前 2 世纪，汉朝使团与商船从徐闻（广东古港）、合浦（广西古港）出海南行，经过两年多的艰难航行，先后到达都元国（今越南南部一带）、邑卢没国（今泰国湄南河口一带）、谌离国（泰国湾西岸一带）、皮宗（新加坡西面之皮散岛）、夫甘都卢国（缅甸安达曼海岸一带）、黄支国（印度东南海岸一带）、已程不国（斯里兰卡）等地；再经过今马六甲海峡，自南洋往北航行，到达日南（越南中部东海岸古港），最后返航回到中国。此后，一条以中国徐闻港、合浦港等港口为起点，连接中国—东南亚—印度洋的海上丝绸之路得到开辟，逐渐形成世界性的贸易网络。

海上丝绸之路开辟的初期，其枢纽在东南亚，后来航线不断延伸，影响也不断扩大。东汉时，中国的商人会聚广州进行贸易，驾船运送丝绸、瓷器经由马六甲和苏门答腊来到印度，并且采购香料、染料运回中国。印度商人则把来自中国的丝绸、瓷器经过红海运往埃及的开罗港，或

漢書卷二十八下
地理志第八下

自日南障塞、徐聞、合浦船行可五月，有都元國，又船行可四月，有邑盧没國，又船行可二十餘日，有諶離國，步行可十餘日，有夫甘都盧國。自夫甘都盧國船行可二月餘，有黃支國，民俗略與珠崖相類。其州廣大，戶口多，多異物，自武帝以來皆獻見。有譯長，屬黃門，與應募者俱入海市明珠、璧流離、奇石異物，齎黃金雜繒而往。所至國皆稟食為耦，蠻夷賈船，轉送致之。亦利交易，剽殺人。又苦逢風波溺死，不者數年來還。大珠至圍二寸以下。平帝元始中，王莽輔政，欲燿威德，厚遺黃支王，令遣使獻生犀牛。自黃支船行可八月，到皮宗；船行可二月，到日南象林界云。黃支之南，有已程不國，漢之譯使自此還矣。

经波斯湾进入两河流域到达安条克（今土耳其南部），再由希腊、罗马商人从埃及的亚历山大、加沙等港口经地中海运往希腊、罗马的大小城邦。与此同时，一些外国使节和商人也沿着海上丝绸之路东来。洛阳是当时的国际性都市。"赛里斯"（Seres）是当时西方人（包括罗马人、粟特人、叙利亚人）对洛阳的称谓，意指中国。去"赛里斯"对他们来说是一件有吸引力且有利可图的事情。东汉和帝时（公元 100 年左右），大秦（古罗马）商团的到来惊动了东汉宫廷。汉和帝欣喜地在洛阳"赐其王金印紫绶"。东汉政府与古罗马的交往此后变得活跃起来，以至汉桓帝延熹九年（公元 166 年）大秦王安敦又"遣使自日南徼外献象牙、

begun launching from Hepu and Xuwen, sailing westwards as they exchanged goods with the Persian merchant ships on the way to Indian Ocean. Gaius Plinius Secundus, scientist of Ancient Rome, made a description in his work *Naturalis Historia* that a large number of merchant ships traveled to and fro between the Apennine Peninsula, Sri Lanka and Seres (China) to trade with each other.

**The Bridge of Sino-Philippines Friendship**
Marking the 600th Anniversary of the Visit to China by the Sultans of Sulu

奎章

纪念苏禄王访华六百周年

## Encyclopedia on Ancient Roman natural science: *Naturalis Historia*

### 《博物志》

盖乌斯·普林尼·塞孔都斯[Gaius Plinius Secundus, 23（或24）—79]，又称老普林尼，古罗马百科全书式的作家，以其所著《博物志》一书闻名。《博物志》发表于公元77年，是对古代自然知识百科全书式的总结，内容涉及天文、地理、动物、植物、医学等科目

赛里斯人，其林中产丝，驰名宇内。丝生于树叶上，取出，浥之以水，理之成丝。后织成锦绣文绮，贩运至罗马。富豪贵族之妇女，裁成衣服，光辉夺目。由地球东端运至西端，故极其辛苦。

——《博物志》

犀角、玳瑁"（《后汉书·西域传》）。此外，安帝永宁元年（公元120年），掸国（今缅甸）王雍由调遣使来汉朝贡，随使团而来的"幻人"（即魔术师）自称是海西（即大秦）人，是由波斯湾或红海乘船经缅甸前来朝贡的（《后汉书·南蛮西南夷列传》）。顺帝永建六年（公元131年），叶调国（今爪哇岛）也派使臣前往中国，与中国进行贸易（《后汉书·南蛮西南夷列传》）。

## Portrayals in Wuliang Ancestral Hall, Han Dynasty (Part)

### 武梁祠汉画像（局部）

山东嘉祥武梁祠的汉画像石刻，曾有题字："璧流离，王者不隐过则至。"由此可见，从印度过来的舶来品璧流离已被中国社会视作宝物

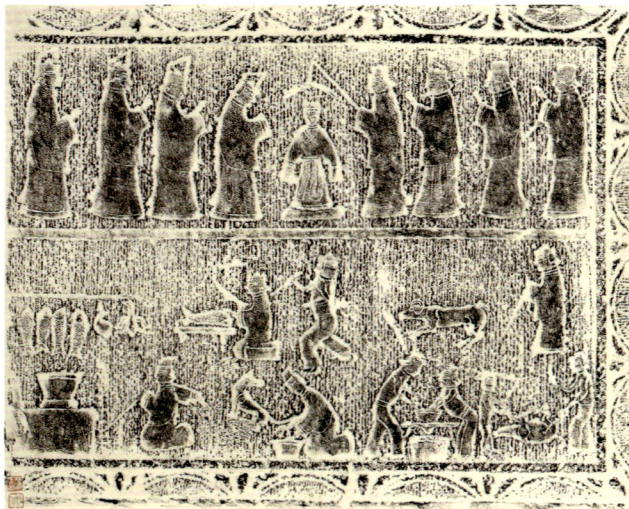

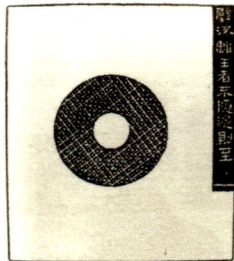

Cultural Relics on Hepu Han Culture Museum Witnessing Maritime Silk Road
汉代海上丝绸之路的历史见证——广西合浦出土的罗马玻璃器、西亚宝石及东南亚金手链（合浦汉代文化博物馆藏）

隋唐时期，中国重新进入"大一统"时代。尤其是盛唐时期，政治、经济、文化等方面都取得很高的成就，唐政府积极推行积极开放、兼容并蓄的对外政策，古老而灿烂的中华文明远播四海。世界各国的国君、使臣、客商、僧侣、学生、工匠等来华访问者络绎不绝。

当时，中国通往东南亚、马六甲海峡、印度洋、红海乃至非洲大陆的航路纷纷开通与延伸。由广州起航，商船经过海南岛，可通往环王国（今越南境内）、门毒国（今越南归仁、芽庄一带）、古笪国（今越南芽庄）、龙牙门（今新加坡和苏门答腊岛之间的林加群岛和海峡）、罗越国（今马来半岛南部柔佛附近）、佛逝国（今苏门答腊东南部）、诃陵国（今印度尼西亚爪哇岛一带）、固罗国（今马来半岛西岸的吉打）、哥谷罗国（今马来半岛克拉地峡西南）、胜邓国（今苏门答腊岛北部棉兰附近）、婆露国（今苏门答腊岛西北部）、狮子国（今斯里兰卡）、南天竺（今印度南部）、婆罗门国（今缅甸西部阿拉干地区和印度阿萨姆邦南部一带）、提罗卢和国（今波斯湾西部阿巴丹附

Nearly 400 years later, Guangzhou Sea Route was developed, which was described in detail in *Geography Chronicles, New History of the Tang Dynasty*. Starting from Guangzhou, the world's famous oriental seaport, the Chinese merchant ships were able to reach the Persian Gulf and the African western coast successfully. From then on, it led to the development of a bustling sea route on the vast waters from Southeast Asian sea to the Indian Ocean. Therefore, the friendly relations between China and the countries along the Maritime Silk Road were strengthened. It was at that time that China began to have the frequent contact with some states on the Philippine Islands.

**The Bridge of Sino-Philippines Friendship**
Marking the 600th Anniversary of the Visit to China by the Sultans of Sulu

纪念苏禄王访华六百周年

近）、乌剌国（今巴士拉东的奥布兰）、大食国（今阿拉伯半岛、伊朗及伊拉克地区）、末罗国（今巴士拉）、三兰国（今东非坦桑尼亚首都达累斯萨拉姆）。这条经南海、印度洋，到达波斯湾各国，远至东非南部的"广州通海夷道"，是 16 世纪以前世界上最长的远洋航线，大大延伸了汉代由徐闻出海的海上丝绸之路，成为连接中国和亚非各国间经济文化交流的纽带。中外使节、商船沿着这条航线穿梭于南海、印度洋、阿拉伯海与红海之间。通过这条通道，中国向外输出了丝绸、瓷器、茶叶和铜铁器四大宗，还有纸张、漆器等；而东南亚的珍珠、玳瑁，印度的宝石、胡椒，中亚和西亚地区的胡椒、亚麻、香料、葡萄、石榴纷纷进入中国。

随着对外贸易的发展，广州成为唐代中国的第一大港、世界著名的东方港市。当时的广州港，"大舶参天""万舶争先"，诗人刘禹锡惊叹之余，曾留下"连天浪静长鲸息，映日帆多宝舶来"的诗句。玄宗开元二年（714 年），在广州设置市舶使，主要负责征税、处置舶货、安排外商的在华贸易，并兼有吸引外商来华贸易之责。除中国人出海经商外，当时汇集广州的各国商人也很多，甚至出现了集中的侨居地。中国著名僧人鉴真和尚在第五次东渡日本时曾途经广州，看到广州"江中有婆罗门、波斯、昆仑等舶，不知其数；并载香药、珍宝，积载如山。其舶深六七丈。师子国、大石国、骨唐国、白蛮、赤蛮等往来居（住），种类极多"（《唐大和上东征传》，为日本奈良时代典籍）。

宋时，中国东南沿海地区商品经济迅速发展，为商人拓展海外贸易提供了坚实的物质基础。同时，造船业走向成熟，当时制造的海船"大者五千料（一料约等于一石，即六十千克），可载五六百人，中者二千料至一千料，亦

During the Song Dynasty, Maritime Silk Road became more and more busy with the development in shipbuilding and navigation. Some Northeast Asian countries such as Korea, Japan as well as Southeast Asian states and Arab states all competed to make trades with China. Owing to its special geographical position, Quanzhou became the central seaport on this run. In 892 A.D., a fighterfrom Mindoro of Philippine islands berthed in Guangzhou, signified its importance as a member of the international trade family.

**Tang Porcelains Founded in Sunk Vessel Heishi**
黑石号出水中国唐代瓷器（"失去的独桅帆船：海上丝绸之路的发现"文物展）

1998年德国打捞公司在印度尼西亚勿里洞岛海域发现了一艘唐代阿拉伯商船沉船，名为"黑石号"。从该船中出水众多文物，仅中国瓷器就达到六万七千多件，其中还有三件完好无损的唐代青花瓷盘和各种金银器、铜镜。2014年12月至2015年4月，加拿大多伦多阿迦汗博物馆与新加坡合作推出"失去的独桅帆船：海上丝绸之路的发现"文物展，展出数百件来自"黑石号"上的中国唐代文物

## Arab Geography Works in Abbasid Dynasty: KITAB.AL-MASALIK. WAL-MAMALIK
### 《道里邦国志》

《道里邦国志》由阿拔斯王朝（即阿拉伯帝国的第二个世袭王朝，古代中国史籍称之为黑衣大食）地理学家伊本·胡尔达兹比赫（820—912）著。该书详细记述亚、非、欧三大洲西起法兰西、西班牙，东至中国、新罗（朝鲜半岛古国之一）、倭国（古日本）、麻逸（菲律宾古国之一，今民都洛岛，或兼指吕宋岛的一部分），北及罗斯（古俄罗斯名），南达印度洋诸岛国的民间风俗、宗教文化、历史遗迹、经济特产及各国之间的路程，描绘出9世纪的国际贸易路线图

从栓府至中国的第一个港口鲁金（Luqin，即唐代的龙编，今越南河内），陆路、海路皆为一百法尔萨赫。在鲁金，有中国石头、中国丝绸、中国的优质陶瓷，那里出产稻米。从鲁金至汉府（Khanfu，即广州），海路为四日程，陆路为二十日程。汉府是中国最大的港口，汉府有各种水果，并有蔬菜、小麦、大麦、稻米、甘蔗。从汉府至汉久（Khanju，可能是泉州）为八日程。汉久的物产与汉府同。从汉久至刚突（Qantu，江都郡，即扬州）为二十日程。刚突的物产与汉府、汉久相同。中国的这几个港口，各临一条大河，海船能在这大河中航行。这些河均有潮汐现象。在刚突的河里可见到鹅、鸭、鸡。中国海疆的长，即从艾尔玛碧勒（Armabil）起始，终至另一端有两个月行程。

——《道里邦国志》

可载二三百人"（《梦粱录》）。此外，中国人已懂得利用季风航行，"每遇冬汛北风发舶"，"夏汛南风回帆"（《通制条格》）。北宋时，航海技术实现重大突破——指南针被运用于航海，"舟师识地理，夜则观星，昼则观日，阴晦观指南针"（《萍洲可谈》），到南宋时"舟舶往来，惟以指南针为则"（《诸蕃志》），这就为航海活动从原来的近海岸航行发展到深洋直航提供了技术保证。从此，海船从中国到东南亚以及印度洋诸国的航行时间大大缩短，更多的中国商人扬帆远航，开辟海外贸易市场。宋朝出口货物达四百多种，其中不乏宝石、工艺品和布匹、皮货、杂货、药材

等生活日用商品。丝绸、陶瓷、茶叶则成为海上丝绸之路贸易中最热销的"三大件"。随着海外贸易的繁荣，大量宋朝铜钱也流往海外，"钱本中国宝货，今乃与四夷共用"（《宋史·食货志》），且"蕃夷得中国钱分库藏贮，以为镇国之宝。故入蕃者非铜钱不往，而蕃货亦非铜钱不售"（《宋会要辑稿·刑法二》）。

与此同时，海外商人纷至沓来。当时，通过海路来到中国进行贸易的客商来自交趾（今越南北部）、占城（今越南中南部一带）、真腊（今柬埔寨）、蒲甘（今缅甸境内）、渤泥（一作勃泥，位于加里曼丹岛北部，今文莱）、阇婆（今印度尼西亚爪哇岛或苏门答腊岛）、三佛齐（今苏门答腊岛）、大食（古阿拉伯帝国）、层拔（今索马里以南）、朝鲜、日本等国。海外诸国商船云集于中国南方各大港口，帆影蔽日，蔚为壮观。曾官至朝廷副相的李邴在目睹泉州海外交通贸易盛况后有"苍官影里三洲路，

**Sunk Vessel Excavated in Houzhu port, Quanzhou, Fujian**
**福建泉州后渚港挖掘宋代沉船**（摄于1974年，福建泉州海外交通史博物馆提供）

宋代泉州造船业发达，有"泉船"之称。1974年，泉州后渚港古码头遗址发现一艘南宋海船，船内出土大批香料、胡椒等货物

*Riverside Scene at Qingming Festival* (Part)

《清明上河图》（局部）

通过汴河等水道，繁荣的海上丝绸之路给北宋都城汴梁带来了琳琅满目的商品：波斯的地毯，天竺的玉器，朝鲜的金器、银器、人参，日本的笔墨、折扇、宝刀，交趾、占城的驯象、驯犀、象牙，三佛齐的琉璃器、琥珀、金刚钻、蒲端的龙脑、丁香，大食的珍珠、通犀，可谓应有尽有，数不胜数。《清明上河图》描绘了以拱桥为中心的汴河及其两岸运输和贸易的忙碌情景

涨海声中万国商"句，描绘的正是海上丝绸之路最亮丽的风景。显然，宋代中国的"万国通商"要比唐代的"万国来朝"具有更开放的大格局。

由于对外贸易兴盛，北宋政府在重要口岸如广州、泉州兴建蕃坊，供外商居住，挑选有威望的外商担任蕃长，并授予相应的官衔。蕃长负责管理蕃坊内部事务，召集外商来华贸易（参见《萍洲可谈·蕃坊蕃商》）。宋太祖开宝四年（971年），设市舶司于广州，专门掌管海外贸易的各种事务，逐渐加强了对市舶贸易的管理。以后，又陆续在杭州、明州（治今宁波市）、泉州以及密州（今山东诸城）、秀州（今浙江嘉兴一带）设置市舶司或市舶务。南宋时期，又增设了温州、江阴两处市舶务。所谓市舶司，

宋史卷一百八十六

食货下八

开宝四年，置市舶司于广州，后又於杭、明州置司。凡大食、古逻、阇婆、占城、勃泥、麻逸、三佛齐诸蕃并通货易，以金银、缗钱、铅锡、杂色帛、瓷器，市香药、犀象、珊瑚、琥珀、珠琲、镔铁、鼊皮、瑇瑁、玛瑙、车渠、水精、蕃布、乌樠、苏木等物。

"掌蕃货、海舶、征榷、贸易之事，以来远人，通远物"（《宋史·职官志》）。

随着宋代海外交通的发展，人们对海外世界的认识也有了显著的提高。当时，不少著作都涉及中外往来与海外世界，如朱彧的《萍洲可谈》、范成大的《桂海虞衡志》和《吴船录》、周辉的《清波别志》、赵彦卫的《云麓漫钞》、岳珂的《桯史》、吴自牧的《梦粱录》、

Thus, for over a thousand years, the Maritime Silk Road opened in the Han Dynasty became more and more bustling after its development. It was until the Ming Dynasty when the world trade began. On the one hand, the Chinese specialties such as tea, silk and porcelain as well as the farming technology like the compass were all shipped to the different areas of the world. Some eminent monks, scholars, artists and translators began to have cultural dialogues with China by means

*The Records of Vassal States,* masterpiece of the Song Dynasty on the foreign geography
《诸蕃志》

宋代海外地理名著，赵汝适著。该书上卷记载海外诸国的风土人情，包括占城国、真腊国、蒲甘国、三佛齐国、大秦国、大食国、麻嘉国、勃泥国、麻逸国、三屿国、蒲哩鲁国、流求国、新罗国、倭国等五十八个古国。下卷记载海外诸国的物产资源，包括乳香、沉香、丁香、肉豆蔻、槟榔、椰子、椰心簟、木香、白豆蔻、胡椒、琉璃、猫儿睛、象牙、犀角、鹦鹉、龙涎、黄蜡等，共五十四篇

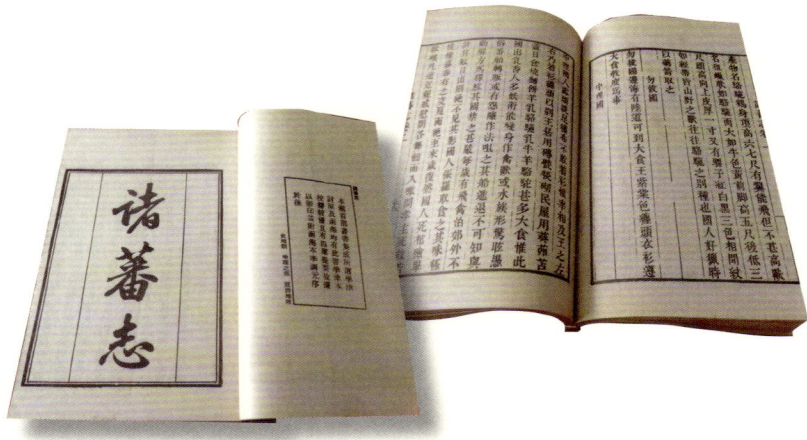

of this sea route. Quoting Chinese President Xi Jinping, he said on the Belt and Road Forum "for International Cooperation, the Ancient Silk Road spanned the Nile River, Tigris and Euphrates River, Indus and the Ganges River, Yellow River and Changjiang River, that crossed through the Egyptian Civilization, Babylon Civilization, Indian Civilization and Chinese Civilization. It also traveresed over Buddhist, Christians and Muslim residential areas. The different civilizations, the different religions and the different races seek common ground while respecting their differences. They are open and inclusive,

周密的《癸辛杂识》等。同时，还有一些记载海外交通的专著出现，如《宣和奉使高丽图经》《岭外代答》《诸蕃志》等，都是反映宋代中国人海外知识的代表作。

有元一代，元政府在经济上采用重商主义政策，鼓励海外贸易，并制定了堪称中国历史上第一部系统性的外贸管理法则。当时海外贸易的范围，东起朝鲜、日本，南到东南亚，西南通印度半岛和西亚，西达非洲和地中海沿岸国家，西北至东欧和俄罗斯，可谓"中国之外，四海维之。海外夷国以万计，惟北海以风恶不可入，东西南数千万里，皆得梯航以达其道路，象胥以译其语言"（《岛夷志略校释》）。元人汪大渊在《岛夷志略》中所记载的海外国家接近一百个，而陈大震《南海志》中所列举的海外地名则为一百四十多个。无论是通商地域之广，还是通商国家之多，元朝都已超过前代，海上丝绸之路进入鼎盛阶段。

这样，开辟于汉代的海上丝绸之路，经过一千多年的发展，日益繁盛，在明代以前即已构建出一个世界贸易的

The Yuan Dynasty Hat with Dragon Design, Mounted with Gold and Diamond
金镶宝石白玉镂空云龙纹帽顶

2001年出土于湖北省钟祥市长滩镇大洪村龙山坡梁庄王墓。梁庄王（1411—1441），名朱瞻垍，明仁宗朱高炽第九子。该帽顶为元朝皇室遗物，覆莲形底座上镶嵌的七颗宝石为产自波斯的松石

网络。一艘艘大船从中国东南沿海的港口启程，扬帆远航，将丝绸、瓷器、茶叶等带往世界各地的同时，也带去了农耕及手工业技术和指南针；而搭乘商船穿梭于这条海上通道的高僧、学者、画师、译者更是文化交融的使者，开展着中国与海外世界的科学技术、思想文化的对话。正如中国国家主席习近平在"一带一路"国际合作高峰论坛上指出："古丝绸之路跨越尼罗河流域、底格里斯河和幼发拉底河流域、印度河和恒河流域、黄河和长江流域，跨越埃及文明、巴比伦文明、印度文明、中华文明的发祥地，跨越佛教、基督教、伊斯兰教信众的汇集地，跨越不同国度和肤色人民的聚居地。不同文明、宗教、种族求同存异、开放包容，并肩书写相互尊重的壮丽诗篇，携手绘就共同发展的美好画卷。古丝绸之路绵亘万里，延续千年，积淀了以和平合作、开放包容、互学互鉴、互利共赢为核心的丝绸之路精神，这是人类文明的宝贵遗产。"

showing respect to each other and depict the wonderful future hand in hand together. The ancient Silk Road spans thousands of miles and years. It forges its core spirit: peace, cooperation, openness, inclusiveness, learning together, drawing lessons from each other, which are mutually beneficial and a win-win situation for all. This is the common precious inheritance of human civilization."

# *Friendly Relations between China and Philippines before the Ming Dynasty*

## 源远流长——明代以前的中菲友好往来

The Philippine Islands are located in the western Pacific Ocean, scenic and abundant. The Batan Islands on the northern most part, and Taiwan Island of China are separated by the Bashi Channel, with a distance of only 67 nautical miles.

During the Tang Dynasty, development of shipbuilding, navigation, and sailing became a trend. The Chinese people living along the southeast coast often navigated to the Philippine Islands to trade with the natives. In the recent

美丽富饶的群岛之国菲律宾，位于亚洲东南部的太平洋面，其最北端的巴坦群岛与中国的台湾省只隔着宽约六十七海里的巴士海峡。中菲两国一衣带水，隔海相望。

但中菲之间的直接交通、通商要晚于东南亚的其他国家和地区，这主要是因为在航海技术尚不成熟的时期，深海航行远不如近海航行安全。至迟到唐代，随着造船技术的进步，航海知识的增加，出海远航形成风气。再加上贸易上的厚利，闽粤沿海居民，常成群结队，扬帆至菲律宾一带。近年来，在菲律宾群岛许多地方发掘出大量唐代古钱币和陶瓷器，甚至还发现了唐代（7世纪中叶）的中国古墓。这说明当时中菲两国的经济交流已相当频繁，甚至有华侨在菲律宾定居经商。

到了宋代，中国与东南亚诸国的海上交通得到进一步发展，其中最突出的成果就是开通了从泉州到渤泥的航线。渤泥国，"去占城与摩逸（一作麻逸，今菲律宾民都洛岛）

**Stone Vessel in Neolithic Age**（Wenzhou Museum）
新石器时代晚期的有段石锛
（现藏于温州博物馆）

有段石锛是新石器时代的造船工具，其分布区域十分广泛。20世纪上半叶，在菲律宾及中国东南部地区相继发现大量有段石锛。这些属于新石器时代的有段石锛，从形态上看极其相似，几乎难以区别。考古界据此推断，上古先民从中国的东南沿海逐岛漂航，来到了菲律宾群岛，并与当地人在生产与文化方面交流融合

Chinese Ancient Porcelain Found in the Philippines
（Dezhou Sulu Culture Museum）
菲律宾出土的中国古代瓷器（德州苏禄文化博物馆藏）

各三十日程，皆计顺风为则"（《宋史·外国五》）。这使得宋政府经渤泥与菲律宾群岛上一些古国和古部落的交往更为密切。宋政府在泉州设立市舶司，允许私人对外贸易，福建沿海与菲律宾之间即有商人冒风涛之险，进行以货易货的交易。起初只是中国商人冒险去菲律宾，后来也有菲律宾各岛岛民随商船来到中国。《宋史·外国五》载："又有摩逸国，太平兴国七年（982年），载宝货至广州海岸。"这是关于中菲关系第一个官方的明确可靠的文字记录。此后，中菲贸易稳步发展。据南宋宁宗年间出任福建路市舶司兼权泉州市舶使的赵汝适所撰《诸蕃志》记载，当时中国商人已与菲律宾的摩逸、三屿（今加麻延、巴拉望、巴吉弄）、蒲里噜（今马尼拉）、白蒲延、苏禄等国有正常的贸易关系。中国商人用瓷器、货金、铁鼎、乌铅、白锡、五色琉璃珠、铁针、皂绫、缬绢、伞等，与当地人交易土产，如黄蜡、吉贝（木棉）、贝纱、真珠、玳瑁、药槟榔、于达布、椰心簟（用椰心草织成的席子）等。除商品贸易外，双方还有官方往来。蒲端国（今菲律宾棉兰老岛东北部）于宋真宗咸平六年（1003年）、景德元年（1004年）、景德四年（1007年）、大中祥符四年（1011年）四次来华。

years, a large number of the Tang Dynasty coins and porcelains, even the Tang Tombs have been found in the Philippines. This shows the close commercial ties between the two countries at that time. It is also evidenced by the number of overseas Chinese who settled there for business.

In the Song Dynasty, the maritime traffic between China and Southeast Asia was much improved. The most noticeable sea route from Quanzhou to Borneo at that time was opened. This promoted the closer ties between the Song Dynasty and the Philippines. Government set customhouses in Quanzhou and permitted the private trade. Besides the commercial ties, there are official exchanges between two governments, for example, Bu-tu-

諸蕃志　〔宋〕趙汝适

麻逸國，在渤泥之北；團聚千餘家，夾溪而居。土人披布如被，或腰布蔽體。有銅佛像，散布草野，不知所自。盜少。商舶入港，駐於官場前。官場者，其國闤闠之所也，登舟與之雜處。酋長日用白傘，故商人必賫以爲贐。交易之例，蠻賈叢至，隨笯籠搬取物貨而去。初若不可曉，徐辨認搬貨之人，亦無遺失。蠻賈迺以其貨轉入他島嶼貿易，率至八九月始歸。以其所得準償舶商，亦有過期不歸者，故販麻逸舶回最晚。三嶼、白蒲延、蒲里嚕、里銀、東流新、里漢等，皆其屬也。土產黃蠟、吉貝、真珠、瑇瑁、藥檳榔、于達布，商人用甆器、貨金、鐵鼎、烏鉛、五色琉璃珠、鐵針等博易。

an paid visits to China for four times between the years 1003 to 1011 A.D.

When the Yuan Dynasty came, the exchanges between two countries became more frequent. The merchant ships from Three Islands (Jamayan, Balaoyou and Bajinong) often came to Quanzhou with their specialty products such as pearls and turtle shells that were popular with the Chinese. At the same time,the merchants of the Yuan Period also frequently went to

如景德四年，蒲端国国王遣使来华，贡物有"玳瑁、龙脑、带枝丁香、丁香母及方物"，北宋政府则"赐冠带、衣服、器币、缗钱有差"。(《宋会要辑稿·蕃夷四》)

元代，中国与菲律宾群岛诸国的交往十分频繁，贸易进一步扩大。如三屿国的商船经常到泉州贸易，品质上等的珍珠、玳瑁等南洋特产深受中国人的欢迎。同时，元朝商人也经常前往苏禄、蒲里噜等地进行贸易。元朝商人对于麻逸商人的信誉印象深刻："蛮贾议价领去博易土货，然后准价舶商。守信事终如始，不负约也。"(《岛夷志略校释》)随着双方交往的频繁，中国的风俗文化在菲律宾逐渐流行。菲律宾男子喜文身，其岛民至泉州以高价文身，只是因为泉州匠人文身技艺较精湛，欲炫耀于他人；岛民从中国返回菲律宾后，也常使人另眼相待。

在明代以前，尤其是在唐、宋、元三代，中菲两国人民有了较为密切的贸易和物质文化交流。一方面，固然是因为唐宋以来，中国经济重心逐渐由黄河流域南移至长江流域，为南方海外贸易的开展提供了有利条件，并且造船与航海技术有了很大进步，使远洋航行成为可能。另一方面，中菲贸易的发展与海上丝绸之路的繁荣密切相关。当时中国与阿拉伯、波斯等国商贸往来频繁，东南亚因地处两者之间，逐渐形成三个区域贸易中心，"正南诸国，三佛齐其都会也；东南诸国，阇婆其都会也；西南诸国，浩乎不可穷，近则占城、真腊为窆里诸国之都会"（《岭外代答》）。菲律宾群岛均在此三大贸易中心的外围，因而不时有阿拉伯、中国等国的商船由阇婆、三佛齐转赴菲律宾群岛进行贸易。因此，在海上丝绸之路兴盛的大环境下，处于南海近旁的菲律宾自然获得了与中国发展贸易关系的机遇。

而阿拉伯、中国等国商人在菲律宾的活动，也推动了菲律宾土著居民往来各岛进行转贩贸易，增加了各岛间的相互了解与联系，这也正是菲律宾群岛走向统一的开始。对内、对外贸易联系的加强，正是这一时期菲律宾群岛发展的特点之一，以至于有菲律宾史学家将十至十六世纪的菲律宾历史称为"贸易与联系的时代"。

岛夷志略 〔元〕汪大渊

男子尝附舶至泉州经纪，罄其资囊，以文其身。既归其国，则国人以尊长之礼待之，延之上坐，虽父老亦不得与争焉。习俗以其至唐，故贵之也。

Sulu and Pulihuan (near present-day Manila) mainly to exchange goods with the natives.

It is clear that the trade and cultural exchanges between Sino-Philippines have a long history together.

# Chapter II
# Sulu Sultans' Visit to China during Yongle's Period

Ancient China had set up a wide trade network through the development of the Tang, Song and Yuan Dynasty, extending to Korea, Japan, Southeast Asia, India Peninsula, West Asia, Africa and some countries along the coast of the Mediterranean. Consequently, the relationship between China and the Philippines changed significantly at the early period of Ming Dynasty. During this age, the maritime communication and commercial exchanges between the two countries reached its climax. Both greatly promoted the bilateral diplomatic ties, and the largest scale mission to China led by three Sultans in the 15th year of the reign of Emperor Yongle (1417 A.D.) was the best example.

# 第二章

## 慕义远来
### ——明代永乐年间苏禄王率团访华

古代中国历经唐、宋、元三代的发展，已经建立起一个东起朝鲜、日本，南到东南亚，西南通印度半岛和西亚，西达非洲和地中海沿岸国家的贸易网络。处于这一世界性贸易网络中的中菲关系，到明代初期发生了重大转变。明初中国与菲律宾的海上交通、贸易往来超越前代而达到高潮，不仅菲律宾群岛各国来华贸易次数增多，与之相伴的是政治外交也大放异彩，尤以永乐十五年（1417年）苏禄三王亲率使团访华的规模最大。

**The Bridge of Sino–Philippines Friendship**
Marking the 600th Anniversary of the Visit to China by the Sultans of Sulu

纪念苏禄王访华六百周年

# The Ming Government and its Peaceful Diplomatic Policy

## 怀柔远人——明政府推行和平的外交政策

In 1368 A.D., the Ming Dynasty was founded. The envoys and merchants from the different states benefited a lot from the Ming's peaceful diplomatic policy and they all admired its prosperity and mightiness. Undoubtedly, Zheng He's Voyages made Ming's fame much further, which attracted some monarchs of the states and tribe heads to travel across the ocean to China one after another to pay tributes. Consequently, the foreign goods and local products flooded into China.

公元 1368 年，明朝建立，明太祖朱元璋励精图治，使明朝政治清明、经济发展，史称"洪武之治"。明太祖为了对外展现大明王朝统一、富强、和平的泱泱大国形象，不断向朝鲜、日本、安南（今越南）、占城、琉球、爪哇（今印度尼西亚爪哇岛一带）、暹罗（今泰国）以及西亚诸国派遣使节。他以"仁、义、礼、智、信"为外交政策的指导思想，坚持以和为贵，怀柔远人，向各国宣传自明朝建国之后"列郡之讴歌四集，百年之污染一新"，并向各国统治者阐明明朝"顷者克平元都，疆宇大同，已录王统"，希望与各国无论远近，"相安于无事，以共享太平之福"。（《明太祖实录》）为打消周边国家对明朝的恐惧心理，明太祖宣布除蒙古以外包括朝鲜、日本、安南等在内的周边十六国为"不征之国"，对周边国家礼遇有加。他反复向外国宣传"朕仿前代帝王治理天下，惟欲中外人民咸乐其所，又虑汝等僻在远方，未悉朕意，故遣使者往谕，咸使闻知"。（《明太祖实录》）这种积极、持重的对外政策，奠定了明朝和平外交政策的基调。因此，"太祖高皇帝时，诸番国遣使来朝，一皆遇之以诚。其以土物来市易者，悉听其便。或有不知避忌而误干宪条，皆宽宥之，以怀远人"（《明太宗实录》）。

经过数十年的休养生息，明朝社会蒸蒸日上，国力更加强盛。1402 年，明成祖朱棣登基，他大力发展经济，提倡文教，使得国家大治，史称"永乐盛世"。在外交方面，明成祖继续推行"以宣德化而柔远人"的对外政策。他以自信开放的胸怀，施行"君万邦，抚四海，厚往薄来"的措施。所谓"厚往薄来"，就是用丰厚的赏赐与尊隆的封号来安抚海外朝贡的国家，回赐之物的价值远远高于进贡之物。"怀夷柔远、厚往薄来"，主观目的是为了展示中国之富强、天子之恩泽惠及四海，使各国心悦诚服、前来朝贡，但客观上促进了中外政治友好、文化交流和朝贡贸易的开展。明成祖对待来华的外国使节，除了高价收买他们携带的货物外，还赏赐给珠宝、酒肉、粮食、衣物等，经常举行宴会款待；对待外国客商，经常减免其商税，告诫本国官员不得与他们争利。明成祖对外宣布："今四海一家，正

**Zheng He's Image**
**郑和画像**

郑和，本姓马，名和，曾因在靖难之役立下战功，被赐姓郑，并升任内宫监正四品太监。永乐三年至宣德八年间，他七次奉命远航西洋，深化了大明帝国与南海及东非诸国之友好关系

## Ruins of Nanjing Longjiang Shipyard, Early Period of the Ming Dynasty
### 龙江宝船厂遗址

明代造船业较前代更为发达，出现了不少著名的造船基地。如明初洪武年间就在今南京市郊上新河建立了"宝船厂"，所造的船称作"宝船"。此外，在福建建造的称作"福船"，在广东建造的称作"广船"。龙江宝船厂建造郑和下西洋所需大型宝船

当广示无外，诸国有输诚来贡者听。尔其谕之，使明知朕意""商税者，国家以抑逐末之民，岂以为利？今夷人慕义远来，乃欲侵其利，所得几何？而亏辱大体万万矣！"（《明太宗实录》）

为了宣扬大明威德、展示中华富强，也为了加强对外友好，深化同各国的政治、经济、文化联系，明成祖派出庞大使团出访沿海各国。永乐元年（1403年）九月，明

## *Zheng He's Sailing Map*（Part）
### 《自宝船厂开船从龙江关出水直抵外国诸蕃图》（局部）

明代重要军事著作《武备志》收录有《自宝船厂开船从龙江关出水直抵外国诸蕃图》，因其名冗长，后人简称为《郑和航海图》。该图绘制的时间大约在1425年至1430年间，是在继承前人航海经验的基础上，以郑和船队的远航实践为依据，经过整理加工绘制而成，对后人研究中国古代航海史和亚非航线的开辟起到了重要作用

成祖派中官马彬等人出使诏谕爪哇、苏门答腊诸蕃国王，并赐以文绮、纱罗等物。十月，又遣中官尹庆、副使闻良辅等出使满剌加（今马六甲）、爪哇、苏门答腊及西洋琐里、柯枝（今印度西南部柯钦一带）、古里（今印度西南部喀拉拉邦一带）等国。永乐三年（1405 年）六月，明成祖命郑和为使、王景弘为副使，率领一支由六十二艘船组成的船队，载有将士二万七千八百余人和大量金、帛、货物，组成历史上空前庞大的使团，出使南洋群岛及印度洋一带。至宣德八年（1433 年），郑和船队一共七下西洋，历时二十八年之久，先后访问了东南亚、南亚、西亚及非洲东海岸三十多个国家和地区，每到一处便宣谕皇帝诏书，向各国君王颁赐印绶、冠服、礼品，吸引招徕各国到明朝访问，扩大中国与海外各国友好通商。

郑和七下西洋是中国古代规模最庞大、船只最多、海员最多、时间最久的海上航行，也是世界航海史上最伟大的创举。航海活动展示了明朝的强盛，也极大促进了中国同世界各国的联系和交往。

明史卷三百四

列傳第一百九十二

宦官一

（鄭）和經事三朝，先後七奉使，所歷占城、爪哇、真臘、舊港、暹羅、古里、滿剌加、渤泥、蘇門答剌、阿魯、柯枝、大葛蘭、小葛蘭、西洋瑣里、瑣里、加異勒、阿撥把丹、南巫里、甘把里、錫蘭山、喃渤利、彭亨、急蘭丹、忽魯謨斯、比剌、溜山、孫剌、木骨都束、麻林、剌撒、祖法兒、沙里灣泥、竹步、榜葛剌、天方、黎伐、那孤兒，凡三十餘國。所取無名寶物，不可勝計。……故俗傳三保太監下西洋，爲明初盛事云。

奎章

纪念苏禄王访华六百周年

**The Bridge of Sino-Philippines Friendship**
Marking the 600th Anniversary of the Visit to China by the Sultans of Sulu

In the early Ming Period, Philippines was not yet called Philippines. It was not a unified country as we know today. They had some independent states and tribes, big and small. However, they have had a close contact with China before the Ming Dynasty. During the Hongwu and Yongle Period, particularly after Zheng He's Voyages, the Sino-Philippines relationship stepped into a new stage. The mutual communication in politics, economy and culture unprecedentedly flourished and the Philippines, specifically Sulu, dispatched their envoys to China many times.

Aside from the frequent political interaction, the relations between China and the Philippines in trade, society and culture became closer and closer. Varieties of goods from China such as farm animals, farming tools, iron wares, lead, white tin, gunpowder,bronze, porcelains, silk fabrics, tamtam, blue cloth, colorful red cloth and so forth were all shipped to the Philippines. On the other hand, some Philippine local products like pearls, turtle shells, gold, dalbergia wood, areca nut, cotton, ceiba, cotton cloth, bamboo cloth, sapanwood and coconut appeared on the Chinese market by

明政府推行"怀夷柔远、厚往薄来"的和平外交政策，使各国使节和商人从明朝的"重义轻利"中得到巨大实惠。明政府的强盛大气、文明富庶，使许多国家和部落倾心仰慕，因而沿海许多国家纷纷"慕义而来"，"慕圣德而率来"。尤其是郑和下西洋后，各国使节接踵而至，不绝于路，一些国君或部落首领还亲自远涉重洋前来朝贡，一度出现"万国来朝"的盛况。各国商品、物产也源源不断进入中国。"自是蛮邦绝域，前代所不宾者，亦皆奉表献琛，接踵中国。或躬率妻孥，梯航数万里，面谒阙庭。殊方珍异之宝，麒麟、狮、犀、天马、神鹿、白象、火鸡诸奇畜，咸充廷实。天子顾而乐之，益泛海通使不绝。"（《明史稿·郑和传》）

明代初期，菲律宾群岛地广人稀，散处着若干大大小小的古国和部落，互不统属，尚未形成统一的国家。明代以前，一些古国和部落已经同中国有着较为密切的往来。明朝洪武、永乐年间，尤其是郑和下西洋前后，中菲关系进入一个新的阶段，明政府同菲律宾群岛诸国的政治、经济、文化交流空前繁荣。

大明太宗文皇帝實錄

永樂四年八月丁酉○東洋馮嘉施蘭土酋嘉馬銀等來朝，賜鈔幣有差。

永樂六年七月辛未○東洋馮嘉施蘭頭目玳瑁·里欲各率其屬來朝，貢方物，賜玳瑁等二人鈔各一百錠、文綺六表裹，餘賜資有差。

吕宋（位于今吕宋岛马尼拉一带）于洪武五年（1372年）至永乐八年（1410年）间三次遣使入华。合猫里（位于今菲律宾群岛东北）于永乐三年（1405年）遣使入贡。冯嘉施兰（位于今菲律宾中部）自永乐四年（1406年）至永乐八年（1410年）其国王三次亲率使团来华访问。古麻剌朗（位于今菲律宾棉兰老岛）国王剌义亦敦奔于永乐十八年（1420年）亲率使团入华，翌年归国，病逝于福建；古麻剌朗国王剌必等于永乐二十二年（1424年）再次遣使入贡，以巩固双方关系。

中菲两国在频繁政治互动的同时，经济贸易和社会、文化交流也日益密切。中国的远洋商船自泉州南下，经海南岛以东洋面，沿越南东海岸南下可达占城、真腊，直下马来半岛、苏门答腊、爪哇、马六甲；转东而行，可抵菲律宾群岛的三屿、麻逸、加麻延、白蒲延、蒲哩噜和苏禄群岛。来自中国的耕畜、耕具、铁器、铅、白锡、火药、青铜、瓷器、绸缎、绫绢、铜锣、蓝布、五彩红布等，大量运往菲律宾；而菲律宾的土特产黄蜡、珍珠、玳瑁、金、降真香、槟榔、棉花、木棉、棉布、竹布、苏木、椰子等，也源源不断地运往中国。这种贸易往来，既扩大了中国商品的市场，刺激了国内生产，也将菲律宾的特产带到中国，丰富了中国百姓的物质文化生活。与此同时，中国的农业、手工业生产技术大量传入菲律宾，推动了菲律宾经济的发展。此外，中国的制度、文化、风俗也随着经贸往来传播到海外，加强了菲律宾人对中国的了解，加深了他们对中华文化的向往。

明經世文編 卷四三三 〔明〕陳子龍等輯
報取回吕宋囚商疏

吕宋本一荒島，魑魅龍蛇之區，徒以我海邦小民，行貨轉販，外通各洋，市易諸夷，十數年來，致成大會，亦有我壓冬之民，教其耕藝，治其城舍，遂成隩區，甲諸海國。

sea. This bilateral commercial exchanges not only satisfied the demand of the domestic market it also enriched the material and cultural life of the Chinese people. It made the Chinese advanced in agricultural and handicraft skills as they exported to the Philippines and promoted its economy. The Chinese political system, cultures and customs were spread to the Philippines, that deepened their understanding and admiration for China and Chinese culture.

**The Bridge of Sino-Philippines Friendship**
Marking the 600th Anniversary of the Visit to China by the Sultans of Sulu

奎章
纪念苏禄王访华六百周年

# The Ancient Sulu and its Relationship with China

## 南洋枢纽——古苏禄国及其与中国的交往

Ancient Sulu was located on the Sulu Archipelago of the Republic of the Philippines. It included the islands of Basilan, Jolo, Tawi-Tawi, Palawan and Zamboanga peninsula and other small islands.

Sulu Archipelago lie near the equator, hot and rainy all year, surrounded with steep cliff along the coast and fertile inland soil. It is rich in aquatic resources because of the shallow and deep waters. It is famous for pearls, sea turtles and corals. Some records about its geographical

古苏禄国位于今天菲律宾共和国的苏禄群岛，包括巴西兰岛、霍洛岛、塔威塔威岛三个主岛及其他小岛。霍洛岛也称和乐岛，旧称苏禄岛，是古苏禄国的政治中心。苏禄群岛地处菲律宾群岛西南、加里曼丹岛东北的苏禄海中，东南隔苏拉威西海和摩鹿加群岛（今马鲁古群岛，属印度尼西亚。因盛产香料，中世纪时被西方称为香料群岛）遥遥相望，由近四百个小岛组成，由东北向西南延伸三百二十多公里。今天古苏禄国的疆域已成为菲律宾共和国的巴西兰省、苏禄省和达维达维省。

苏禄群岛地近赤道，终年湿热多雨。海岸多悬崖峭壁，山深田瘠，不利于农业生产。然而各岛之间为浅海，多珊瑚礁，水产资源丰富，自古以出产珍珠和海龟而闻名于世。明代张燮在《东西洋考》中有关于苏禄的记载："（苏禄）

**Today's Sulu Custom** （Photo by Xu Zuosheng）
苏禄遗风（徐作生拍摄）

Today's Sulu Wate bahay kubo（Photo by Xu Zuosheng）

今苏禄水上高脚屋（徐作生拍摄）

聚落不满千家，山涂田瘠，间植粟麦，民食沙糊、鱼虾、螺蛤。气候半热，男女短发，缠皂缦，系小印布。煮海为盐，酿蔗为酒，编竹为布。时从鲛室中探珠满袖，自成生涯云。"

　　苏禄群岛面积不大，在十四世纪以前经济社会尚不发达，但其地理位置极为重要。它扼中国与阿拉伯、棉兰老岛、维萨亚和婆罗洲（今加里曼岛）之间的交通要冲，是古代海上丝绸之路的枢纽之一，在中菲交往中发挥着纽带作用。

　　古代船舶航行在波涛汹涌的海洋上，需要依靠风力推动。在长期的航海实践中，人们逐渐掌握了太平洋季风（信风）的规律。在夏季，海洋气压高，亚洲大陆气压低，风从海洋吹向大陆，形成西南季风；到冬天，亚洲大陆气压高，海洋气压低，风又从大陆吹向海洋，形成东北季风。航海的人们根据这一规律，冬季从中国东南沿海出发，利用东北季风通过南海到达占城，再沿占城向西南航行到达马六甲，通过马六甲海峡西行可到印度、斯里兰卡，直至阿拉伯。另外，从马六甲向南，越过马六甲海峡，可抵苏门答腊，沿苏门答腊向东到爪哇，由爪哇向北便是婆罗洲。

features and customs can be seen in the inscribed documents of the Ming Dynasty records.

The Sulu Archipelago was a small area and remained undeveloped before the 14<sup></sup>th century. But because of its strategic location, it became an important traffic port between China and Arabia, and Kalimantan Island, and one of the transportation junctions along the Maritime Silk Road. The Chinese merchant ships cannot reach Mait and Luzon without passing by Sulu Archipelago. The western trade vessels carrying perfume also took it as a middle station on the way to Moluccas Islands. Hence, despite how small as it was, Sulu Archipelago

**The Bridge of Sino-Philippines Friendship**
Marking the 600th Anniversary of the Visit to China by the Sultans of Sulu

纪念苏禄王访华六百周年

played a significant role in the above-mentioned routes. As a result its relationship with China was much more frequent than any other states witihin the Philippine Islands.

During Zheng He's Voyages, several contingents and envoys were sent to pay visits to the Southeast Asian countries. One contingent to the Sulu Islands led by Poontaokong was warmly welcomed by the native people. Unfortunately, he died of illness later, and then was buried on the Bayan ng Hill of Jolo Island. His

当时人们习惯以婆罗洲为分界线，称婆罗洲以西为"西洋"、婆罗洲以东为"东洋"。海船经婆罗洲往东北便是苏禄，再以苏禄为中转站，分两条航线：一条航线向北经巴若望、民都洛可达菲律宾北部最大的岛屿——吕宋岛；另一条航线则从苏禄继续向东南行，越过苏拉威西海，可到达盛产香料的摩鹿加群岛。海船返回中国，则需要等到第二年夏季刮西南风的时候，从原路返航。这样，小小的苏禄岛便成为东洋航线的中心，中国的商船到菲律宾群岛的麻逸、毗舍耶、吕宋，必须先经过苏禄；西方商船到摩鹿加群岛去贩运香料，也往往要以苏禄为中间站。因此，苏禄虽小，但在中国与"东洋""西洋"之间的交通往来中担负着重要角色，其与中国的交往反较菲律宾其他地区更为频繁而重要。

近年来，在苏禄岛上不断发现中国晚唐的陶瓷，印证了中国与苏禄交往历史的悠久。元代古籍《大德南海志》（1304年）中记载有"苏录"国名。至大元年（1308年），

東西洋考　蘇禄
〔明〕張燮

舟至彼中，將貨盡數取去，夷人攜入彼國深處售之，或別販旁國，歸乃以夷貨償我。彼國值歲售多珠時，商人得一巨珠攜歸，可享利數十倍。若夷人探珠獲少，則所償數亦倍蕭索，顧逢年何如耳。

元朝曾派使臣访问苏鲁（即苏禄）。（参见《元史·武宗纪》）元人汪大渊作《岛夷志略》、明人张燮作《东西洋考》，均对当时苏禄的地理位置、物产等有较为详细的记述。

郑和下西洋，在访问东南亚过程中，曾派遣使节分路出访，其中一支访问了渤泥（今加里曼丹岛）和苏禄。明人陆容《菽园杂记》卷三载："太监郑和、王景弘、侯显等……由太仓刘家港开船出海，所历诸蕃地面……曰三岛国、曰渤泥国、曰苏禄国。"访问苏禄的使团由白本头（后世尊称本头公）率领，在苏禄群岛主岛——和乐岛登岸，受到当地酋长的热情接待。不幸的是，后来白本头突染重症，病逝于岛上，后被隆重安葬于巴笼山上。本头公墓至今保存完好，香火不断，成为中国与苏禄友好交往的历史见证。

本头公墓旁，还有一座墓葬。墓主人是苏禄当地一位穆斯林酋长，他生前是本头公的好朋友，两人曾滴血为盟，

tomb is still well preserved today and the local Chinese held its memorial every year. There was a grave of a muslim chieftain beside his tomb. Accordingly, they were good friends and the chieftain claimed he would be buried by Poontaokong after his death. This story witnessed the friendship between China and the Philippines. Nowadays we can still find some temples in memory of Poontaokong in the Philippines, Malaysia and Thailand.

**Pentaokong Temple** (Offered by Prof. Darwin Absari, Philippines University)

本头公庙（菲律宾大学Darwin Absari 教授提供）

# The Bridge of Sino-Philippines Friendship
### Marking the 600th Anniversary of the Visit to China by the Sultans of Sulu

奎章

纪念苏禄王访华六百周年

## Gate of Pentaokong Tomb （Offered by Prof. Darwin Absari, Philippines University）

本头公墓山门（菲律宾大学Darwin Absari 教授提供）

## 1. Pentaokong Tomb Passage （Photo by Xu Zuosheng）

本头公墓神道（徐作生拍摄）

## 2. Land God Tablet of Pentaokong Tomb （Photo by Xu Zuosheng）

本头公墓"后土"碑（徐作生拍摄）

### 本头公墓

位于今苏禄省首府和乐市郊外西北方向的山麓，华人称之为巴笼山，山上建有本头公庙。古庙主体建筑早已毁于战火，幸运的是本头公神像被当地百姓从战火中抢救出来。本头公神像系用整块巨木雕成的半身坐像，高一米六，双目炯炯有神，身披黄色战袍。战袍上有白色缎带一幅，上书"新郑白府××××"字，指明本头公的原籍是中国河南新郑。神像底座刻有英文"Pentaokong"（音译为"本头公"）。由本头公庙拾级向上，于蔓青荒草中有茔墓两座，其中一座即本头公墓，现存墓碑为乾隆五十六年（1791年）正月所立，为汉字隶书。墓碑正面刻"正位"两大字，隶书阴刻；反面刻"后土"两大字。

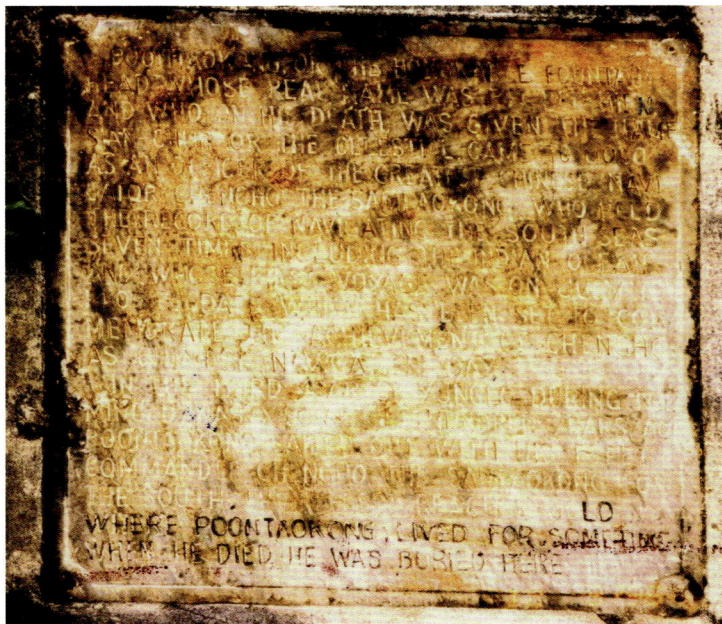

**本头公墓英文碑**

本头公墓碑铭，原有二通，一为汉文，一为英文，由于战争不断，两碑皆佚。后发现另一座被遗弃的英文石碑，其中大半内容可辨析，原文如下：

Poontaokong or the honorable fountain head，whose real name was Pai Poon Hien，and who，on his death，was given the name Sian-chun，or the celestial，came to Jolo as an officer of the greatest Chinese navigator Zheng He the Sampaokong，who held the record of navigating the south seas seven times including the Indian Ocean and whose first voyage was on July 15-date which has been set to commemorate the achievement of Zheng He as Chinese Navigation Day. In the 3$^{rd}$ year of Yunglo during the Ming Dynasty，some-hundred years ago，Poontaokong sailed with his fleet commander Zheng He，the Sampaokong，for the south. Their fleet reached Jolo，where Poontaokong lived for some time. When he died，he was buried here.

译文：本头公，吾苏禄华人之先祖也。公本名曰白本孩（音），升天后被奉若仙君或神灵。本头公生前为中国最伟大之航海家郑和（即三宝公）麾下一名军士，公驾舟南渡至苏禄。三宝公曾创下七下西洋之纪录，此中尚包括印度洋。三宝公首次下西洋为七月十五日也，这一天遂被后人定为中国之航海日，以纪念郑和之功绩。明朝永乐三年，本头公与其宝船主帅三宝公一起，出海向南航行。船队抵达苏禄岛，本头公于岛上居住数年。当其仙逝后，便被埋葬于此

结为兄弟。酋长临终前给族人留下遗言，死后就把他葬在本头公的墓旁。两座墓葬，见证了一段中国与苏禄友好往来的佳话。如今，苏禄人每年都要举行活动纪念本头公。本头公的事迹更是在东南亚各国早已传为佳话。在菲律宾、马来西亚、泰国等国均有本头公庙，香火不断。本头公、本头公庙及本头公在菲后裔，是中菲两国友好交往的历史见证。

**The Bridge of Sino-Philippines Friendship**
Marking the 600th Anniversary of the Visit to China by the Sultans of Sulu

奋章
纪念苏禄王访华六百周年

# Three Sulu Sultans's Visit to China Traveling Across Ten Thousand Miles

## 梯山航海——苏禄三王率使团万里来华

The friendship between China and the Philippines was introduced by Zheng He's Voyages. Moved and inspired by the Ming Government, Paduka Pahala, the Sulu Sultan together with the leaders of other tribes decided to come to China to pay tribute. This was actually their response to reciprocate Zheng He's visits.

In May of the 15th year of Emperor Yongle's Reign during the Ming Dynasty (1417 A.D.), a large scale mission consisting of 340 people led by Paduka Pahala (Sultan of Sulu). Precious presents like pearls, diamond and turtle shells made their way over the rough seas to Beijing to pay tribute to the Ming Dynasty Emperor Yongle.

The mission started from Sulu island and arrived at Quanzhou port in Fujian Province of China in July via Brunei, Malaka and Champa

郑和下西洋、遣使出访苏禄，为中菲两国架起了一道友谊的彩桥。在中外交往空前繁荣的时代潮流下，苏禄东王巴都葛叭答剌久慕中华国力强盛、文化博大精深，决定效仿当时一些国君的做法，率东、西、峒三大部落首领和官员入华访问。这实际上是对郑和使团访问苏禄的回访。

明朝永乐十五年（1417 年）五月，苏禄东国首领巴都葛叭答剌（Paduka Pahala）、西国首领麻哈剌叱葛剌麻丁（Mahala Chigemading）、峒国首领叭都葛巴剌卜（Baduge Balabo），率领眷属陪臣三百四十余人，组成庞大的友好使团，携带珍珠、宝石、玳瑁等礼物，踏上遥远的访华之路。

当时的苏禄群岛，尚未形成统一的伊斯兰苏丹王国，而是存在大大小小的若干部落，这些部落联合起来组成部落联盟，推选力量最强大或才能最出众的酋长为共同领袖。来华访问的苏禄东王巴都葛叭答剌、西王麻哈剌叱葛剌麻丁、峒王叭都葛巴剌卜，可能就是当时苏禄三个大部落的酋长。三人之中，东王巴都葛叭答剌为共同领袖，以他为尊。另一方面，可能由于海岛隔绝的缘故，当地还有一些母系氏族社会的残留。例如，妇女有较高的地位，享有财产继承权，甚至可以继位为部落酋长。在三王访华时，其中的峒王叭都葛巴剌卜就是一位女酋长。

虽然苏禄群岛与中国福建泉州的直线距离不过数千海里，但苏禄使团来华并非直接北上，而是先折向西边后再向北航行，走传统的"东洋航线"，也就是海上丝绸之路航线。当时，帆船出海主要依靠太平洋季风，中国的帆船每年十一、十二月利用东北季风从泉州出发，经广州、占城、满剌加、苏门答腊、阇婆、渤泥到达苏禄，第二年五、六月刮南风时，再按原路返回中国，故当时有"北风航海南风回"的谚语。东南亚各国的帆船前往中国，也大多走这条航线。该航线路远、费时，往返需一年左右的时间。苏禄使团便是于五月利用太平洋的西南季风从苏禄本岛出发，向西航行经过渤泥、满剌加，再往北沿着中南半岛海岸而行，经真腊、占城等地，再折往中国的广州、泉州。经过两个多月的航行，历尽艰辛，跨越万里海波，于七月到达中国福建的泉州港，开始了访问中国的行程。

苏禄三王亲率使团不远万里、不辞艰辛来华访问，可谓"诚贯金石"。在当时的航海条件下，风暴、恶浪、暗礁、险滩、海盗以及辨别航向等，都是巨大的考验。苏禄使团冲破艰难险阻，梯山航海到达中国，这是中外交流史上的壮举，充分体现了中菲人民渴望和睦共处、友好往来的真挚情谊。

strait. The whole journey took more than two months across ten thousand nautical miles. Thus, the visit to China began.

Sulu mission experienced the stormy and wavy weather, dangerous reefs and pirates. It stood the tests of the sea and withstood all kinds of troubles along their journey. They successfully arrived in China. It was a magnificent feat in the world diplomatichistory, fully showing the sincere friendship between two nations, China and the Philippines.

**Sulu Mission Sailing on the High Sea** (Scenes description)
苏禄使团的船队航行在茫茫大海中（场景描绘）

# Chapter III

## A Courteous Reception for the Sulu Mission from the Chinese Emperor

In July, 1417 A.D. (the 15<sup>th</sup> year of the reign of Emperor Yongle), the Sulu mission reached Quanzhou port, Fujian province, China. Compared with the other visiting missions, Sulu mission was by far the largest. The Chinese Emperor was most pleased with their visit. He spoke highly of them, and offered them unprecedented courteous reception. This was the grandest foreign mission Ming government received and Sulu Sultan's visit to China was an important international foreign affair in the history of the world medieval ages. From then on, the communication and relationship between China and the Philippines stepped into a brand new era.

# 厚往薄来

第 三 章

—— 中国皇帝对苏禄使团的礼遇

明永乐十五年（1417年）七月，苏禄使团抵达中国福建泉州港。在当时来华的各国使团中，苏禄使团可谓规模宏大，一路浩浩荡荡，"空国来归，鳞次阙下"（《东西洋考》）。中国皇帝对苏禄使团的到访非常高兴，对苏禄三王高度赞誉，并给予使团空前的礼遇。这是明政府接待的阵容最为壮观的外国使团，是世界中世纪史上一次重要的国际外交活动。从此，中菲交流进入了一个崭新的阶段。

# Grand Reception for the Sulu Mission from the Ming Envoy

## 迎劳宴飨——明朝专使为苏禄使团接风洗尘

When Emperor Zhu Di heard that Sulu mission had disembarked at Quanzhou port, he at once ordered the officials along the way to give them the ceremonial welcome and at the same time sent special envoys to Longjiang Courier Station of Yingtian Prefecture (today known as the Nanjing City) to meet them.

明成祖朱棣得知苏禄使团一行已在福建泉州登岸后，旋即下令沿途地方官员隆重接待，并派专使到应天府（今南京市）龙江驿迎候。

苏禄使团在泉州稍作休整，便沿海北上，由吴淞口入长江，经浏河，到达应天府的龙江驿（今南京鼓楼区境内）。龙江驿官员将苏禄使团迎至驿站，同时上报应天府，由应天知府将苏禄国三位国王送入专掌接待事务的应天会同馆。

The Imperial Envoy Welcoming Sulu Mission at Longjiang Courier Station, Yingtian Prefecture
(Scenes description)

明成祖专使在应天府龙江驿迎候苏禄使团（场景描绘）

Ming Ministers holding a Welcoming Banquet for Sulu Mission at the Imperial Hall, Yingtian Prefecture（Scenes description）
明朝大臣在应天府会同馆举行苏禄使团欢迎宴会（场景描绘）

在会同馆中，明成祖专使以及礼部尚书已奉明成祖的旨意，为苏禄使团准备了盛大的宴会，为三位国王接风洗尘。依照礼制，宴席上，会同馆为苏禄三王设座于正厅的西北，东向；为明成祖专使以及礼部尚书、应天府知府设座于正厅的东南，西向。宴席的招待标准为"茶食五般，按酒五般，果子五般，汤饭一分，酒三钟"（《大明会典》），并有教坊司表演乐舞。

After a short stay in Quanzhou, Sulu mission sailed northwards along the coast, as they entered the Changjiang River from Wusong and arrived at Longjiang Courier Station via the Liuhe River, where the special envoys await. They were sent to Huitong Hotel accompanied by the Governor of Yingtian Prefecture, where a rich dinner was prepared for the visitors from afar.

**The Bridge of Sino-Philippines Friendship**
Marking the 600th Anniversary of the Visit to China by the Sultans of Sulu

金章
纪念苏禄王访华六百周年

# The Chinese Emperor Crowning Sulu Sultan

## 赤绶金章——中国皇帝封赐苏禄三王

Several days later, Sulu mission sailed up along the Grand Canal, passed through the Yangzhou, Xuzhou, Jizhou, Linqing, Dezhou, Cangzhou,Tianjin and Tongzhou and arrived in Beijing in early August.

Seeing such a large scale foreign mission pay tribute, Emperor Zhu Di was so pleased that he offerd them an unprecedented reception at Fengtian Palace.

On one morning of August, solemn air permeated in and out of the imperial palace and the royal guards and the civil and military officials were waiting out of Meridian Gate. Banners fluttering in the air, the guard of honour and bands were all set. The welcoming ceremony was a fine spectacle.

With the accompaniment of bands, Paduka Pahala presented his credentials to Emperor Zhu Di, as well as the precious presents like

苏禄使团稍作休整便离开应天府，由明成祖专使陪同，从浦口沿着京杭大运河北上，经过扬州、徐州、济州、临清、德州、沧州、天津、通州等地，于八月初到达北京。

永乐十五年（1417年）八月辛卯日，明成祖在奉天殿举行了盛大隆重的会见仪式。

明成祖非常重视同苏禄三位国王的会见，给予高规格接待。在会见的前一日，内使监在皇宫正殿奉天殿内陈设御座香案，尚宝司在御座前的大殿正中摆好宫中特制的宝案，侍仪司在午门外安排迎候苏禄使团的诸项事宜等。

八月辛卯日清晨，皇宫内外肃穆庄严，禁卫宫廷的卫队和文武百官整齐地排列在午门外东西两侧。奉天门外旌旗猎猎，拱卫司在丹陛和丹墀东西两侧陈列仪仗，丹墀南侧数十人的乐队和指挥早已准备就绪，场面十分壮观。时辰到，乐师鼓乐，仪仗迎苏禄三位国王及使团成员于午门外，由西门入奉天西门，至殿前丹墀西侧。苏禄三位国王肃然直立，等候与明成祖的会见。此时，明成祖身着最庄严尊贵的礼服——通天冠绛纱袍，在鼓乐声中登上宝座。随后，鼓乐声止。

在奉天殿外，执事官将苏禄使团的礼物放置于苏禄三位国王面前。随后鼓乐再次齐鸣，苏禄三位国王——东国首领巴都葛叭答剌、西国首领麻哈剌叱葛剌麻丁、峒国首领叭都葛巴剌卜及使团成员向明成祖行礼，鼓乐停止。

引导官引导苏禄三位国王进入奉天殿内，鼓乐又大作。东王巴都葛叭答剌代表苏禄三国向明成祖递交"国书"（金缕表文），并赠送从本国带来的珍珠、宝石等珍贵礼品，另外还有苏禄的方物特产梅花脑、米脑、竹布、棉布、玳瑁、降香、苏木、胡椒、荜拔、黄蜡、番锡等，这实际上是向中国介绍了苏禄国内丰富的土特产，是苏禄产品的展示和交流。明成祖则按照中国历代帝王"赐封"的成例，"封巴都葛叭答剌为苏禄国东王，麻哈剌叱葛剌麻丁为苏禄国西王，叭都葛巴剌卜为苏禄国峒王，并赐诰命及袭衣、冠服、印章、鞍马、仪仗。随从头目三百四十余人赐冠带、金织文绮、袭衣有差"（《明太宗实录》卷一九二）。三王之中，以东王为尊。在此过程中，苏禄三王及使团成员一再向明成祖表示感谢。

pearl jewels, and the special presents such as borneol, bamboo cloth, cotton cloth, turtle shell, dalbergia wood, logwood, and black pepper etc. In fact, the rich special products of Sulu were introduced to China in this manner. According to the Chinese royal convention of Emperor Zhu Di, of the three kings, granted Paduka Pahala, Mahala Chigemading and Baduge Balabo, it was Paduka Pahala, the Sulu Sultan of the East Kingdom who was most honored by the emperor.

**Chinese Emperor Receiving Three Sultans at Fengtian Palace**
(Scenes description)

明成祖在奉天殿与苏禄三王举行会见仪式（场景描绘）

蘇祿國。永樂間，賜國王紗帽、金鑲玉帶、鈒花金帶、金蟒龍等衣服，金銀錢鈔、珍珠、錦紵絲、紗羅、器皿、鋪陳等物。王妃冠服、銀錢鈔、紵絲等物。王男女親戚、頭目、使女冠帶、衣服諸物，各有差。

大明會典
給賜二
外夷上

At the same time, the Chinese government presented the gifts in return such as silk, gold, silver, official uniform and seals.

Besides the titles of nobility, the Ming Emperor granted the rich rewards to other members of the mission, which fully embodied the royal conventional generous diplomatic policy.

After meeting with the Emperor Zhu Di in Fengtian Palace, the three Sultans came to Wenhua Palace to pay a visit to the crown princes according to the rules of diplomatic etiquette. And then they called on the other ministers successively.

在苏禄国三位国王中，叭都葛巴剌卜原是"故权苏禄峒者之妻"，苏禄峒国酋长死后，她成为峒国首领。苏禄东王访华时，她审时度势，毅然亲率部属，随同东王一起来到中国，谒见了明成祖，被封为峒王。叭都葛巴剌卜作为一个岛国的女性首领，为了自己国家的利益，远涉重洋，到中国来进行外交政治活动，堪称巾帼女杰、卓越的女外交活动家。明成祖破例封女性为王，这在中国古代史上是绝无仅有的。一方面说明明成祖对苏禄古老风俗是尊重的，另一方面也说明他对苏禄峒王历尽千辛、不远万里来华访问表示敬意。

除了赐封，明成祖还对苏禄使团中的三百余位成员，上至三位国王，中至王妃王子，下至使团中的头目、使女等，均予以不同层次的赏赐。而从赏赐的物品来看，明政府的礼物价值远远高于苏禄使团进贡之物，这充分显示了明政府"厚往薄来"的外交成例，得到苏禄使团的高度赞赏。

苏禄国三位国王会见完明成祖，出了奉天殿后，即按照礼仪到文华殿拜见皇太子。在文华殿正殿，皇太子朱高炽身着皮弁服升座，苏禄三王于殿外行礼，太子立即起身受礼，旋即对三王予以答谢。

在北京期间，苏禄使团还相继拜会了在北京的亲王、内阁大学士、六部尚书等明政府官员。

# The Courteous Reception for the Sulu Mission from the Ming Government

## 宾至如归——明政府热情款待苏禄使团

苏禄王一行在京二十七天，受到明政府空前的礼遇。外宾们享国宴、听雅乐、观杂戏、游名胜，不亦乐乎。

会见仪式结束后，明成祖在谨身殿举行国宴款待苏禄使团，场面盛大，气氛热烈。皇帝、太子、在京诸王及文武百官出席；苏禄东王巴都葛叭答剌、西王麻哈剌叱葛剌麻丁、峒王叭都葛巴剌卜，东王妃葛木宁、东王长子都麻含、东王次子安都鲁、东王三子温哈剌及苏禄从官列席。明成祖坐于谨身殿正中主座，面南背北；太子朱高炽坐于御座东侧，诸王坐于皇太子下首，背东向西。御座西侧主宾为苏禄东王巴都葛叭答剌，下首分别是西王麻哈剌叱葛剌麻丁、峒王叭都葛巴剌卜及王妃、王子。明政府的文武重臣列于第二行、第三行。苏禄从官、明政府三品及以下官员俱以序次坐于殿外西庑。

宴席由礼部官员主持。明成祖身着常服，升御座，大乐鼓吹振作，鸣鞭，鼓乐停止。皇太子朱高炽及诸位亲王各就座，礼部官员引导苏禄国三位国王入位就座。此后，光禄卿举御食案进于御前，礼部侍郎光禄少卿举食案进于皇太子、诸位亲王之前，礼部郎中光禄丞举食案进于苏禄三王之前。文武重臣及苏禄王妃、王子各依次就座。国宴开始。

祝酒、进食等活动皆按国宴礼制进行。内官和鸿胪寺

The Sulu mission stayed in Beijing for 27 days, enjoying the state banquets, wonderful musical accompaniment, the Chinese operas and the traditional acrobatic shows.

After the welcoming ceremony, Emperor Zhu Di with his officials held the state banquet to entertain them in Jinshen Palace. The banquet was hosted by the officials of Ministry of Rites. At the banquet, Emperor Yongle proposed a toast to Sulu Mission, and the guests toasted in returned. The whole palace was full of happiness.

## Chinese Emperor Holding a State Banquet for Sulu Mission at Jinshen Palace (Scenes description)
永乐帝在谨身殿举行国宴招待苏禄使团（场景描绘）

卿依次为明成祖、皇太子、苏禄国三位国王等人斟酒，此时，细乐奏响《太清之曲》。和声郎举手唱"上酒"，明成祖举爵一饮而尽，皇太子、苏禄三王等依次举杯饮酒。饮讫，音乐停止。再斟酒，细乐奏响感皇恩之曲。内使监令进食案于御前，此后依次给皇太子、苏禄三王等上食案。宴席按大宴上桌的标准，"按酒五般，果子五般，烧炸五般，茶食，汤三品，双下大馒头，羊肉饭，酒七钟"。当大乐响起，和声郎即唱上食，明成祖举箸进食，皇太子、苏禄三王等依次进行。如此这般，酒行九轮，食上五品。每一次行酒、品食始终伴随着音乐。音乐响起，即为皇帝和众人依次斟酒、上食，饮讫吃罢，音乐便停止。每一次行酒品食所奏乐章均不相同，各有定制，其中既有气势磅礴的大乐，也有婉约细腻的细乐。行酒品食间除音乐外，还穿插着舞蹈，且百戏承应、杂陈诸戏。在盛大的歌舞声中，整个筵宴洋溢着庄严而祥和的气氛。

谨身殿国宴后不久，皇太子朱高炽又在东宫宴请苏禄王一行。筵宴规格及礼仪均与谨身殿国宴相同。太子坐于殿中主位，苏禄东王、西王、峒王及诸王妃王子坐于西侧宾位，大明诸亲王陪坐于东侧。明政府的六部尚书等大臣列于第二排。苏禄从官及东宫属官坐于西庑。入座后，"酒凡七行，食五品"，其中也穿插着舞乐表演。

东宫宴后，礼部也奉旨分别宴请苏禄使团一行。宴请当日，明政府官员均列仪仗，于门外迎接苏禄三位国王。开席之前，先对三王致以礼待之意，然后入席就座。席间，斟酒作细乐，进食作大乐。整个宴会过程均照"凡酒七行食五品"的规制，并杂陈诸戏。总之，明政府三日一大宴，一日一小宴，盛情款待苏禄贵宾。

除了宴请，礼部官员还在北京会同馆举行招待会，请苏禄使团观赏戏剧表演。明初五大传奇戏曲——《琵琶记》

After the state banquet, the crowned prince, Zhu Gaozhi, held another feast in the East Palace. Afterwards the officials of the Ministry of Rites also entertained them. Accordingly, big feasts were held every three days and small ones every day during their stay in Beijing.

Besides the banquets, Sulu visitors were invited by Ministry of Rites to watch the Chinese classic plays such as *The Story of Pipa, The Story of White Rabbit* and *Baiyueting*. They were all struck deeply by the Chinese wonderful dramatic art.

The officials of the Ministry of Rites showed Sulu guests around Beijing City the following days. They were toured to places where both the high manual technologies and prosperous businesses gave them a deep impression about China.

**Chinese Emperor Holding Reception at the Imperial Hall and Enjoying the Opera with Sultans** (Scenes description)

礼部在会同馆举行招待会，邀请苏禄王观赏戏剧表演（场景描绘）

《荆钗记》《白兔记》《拜月亭》《杀狗记》依次上演。苏禄客人为精彩绝伦的中华戏剧文化所吸引，情不自禁地拍手叫好，个个喜形于色。

在礼部官员的引领下，苏禄贵宾还游览了繁华的北京城。出承天门便是繁华的商业区，沿街店铺林立、旗幡招展，茶楼、酒楼、货栈、会馆、戏楼、书场等星罗棋布，商旅辐辏，车水马龙，熙熙攘攘。杭州府产的精美的绫罗绸缎，苏州府产的工艺绝伦的缂丝彩锦，松江府产的细密轻柔的飞花布，景德镇产的青花瓷、釉里红等，各种商品琳琅满目、应有尽有。高超的手工技艺、繁荣的商业、发达的经济，给苏禄使团一行留下了深刻的印象。此外，苏禄使团还特别到太庙参加谒圣等活动，以及参观大明最高学府国子监和皇家藏书楼文渊阁等处。太庙是配享中国帝王祖先及历代先贤的祠堂。谒圣于太庙是对中国正统政权的认可，是苏禄使团访华的应有之意，象征性的政治意义被寓于轻松的游观之中。国子监可谓当时世界上最大的国家学府，而

Honored Sulu Guests Visiting the prosperous Beijing City (Scenes description)

苏禄贵宾游览繁华的北京城（场景描绘）

文渊阁的早期功用主要是藏书和编书。在游览国子监及文渊阁的过程中，苏禄使团一行被博大精深的中华文化深深吸引，他们也借着此次机会与中国的文人儒士进行了文化上的交流。

在热情接待之余，明政府还在会同馆内与苏禄使团进行货物贸易。依照明成祖的旨意，明政府对随使团船队而来的所有苏禄商品一律给予免税的优惠待遇。苏禄珍珠行销两京（即南京应天府、北京顺天府），深受达官贵族的喜爱。佩戴、把玩苏禄珍珠，一时成为贵族消费的时尚。这也为苏禄带来了丰厚的利润。

其实，苏禄王一行在京期间的具体活动未见于史籍，但二十七天的行程足以为今人提供丰富的想象空间。

At the same time, the bilateral exchanges of goods were carried out. In the light of Zhu Di's order, all the goods carried by Sulu mission were duty free. Their pearls were popular with Chinese nobles and adorning them became a fad, which also brought the great benefit to Sulu delegation.

# Sulu Mission Return with Honors

## 陛辞而归——苏禄使团载誉归国

The 27-day stay in Beijing witnessed excellent Chinese culture and the unprecedented courteous reception to Sulu mission. On last day of August of the fifteenth year (1417 A.D.) of Emperor Yongle's reign, the Sulu delegation accomplished thier diplomatic mission and successfully ended the visit to China. Paduka Pahala, Mahala Chigemading and Baduge Balabo, bid farewell to Emperor Yongle and sailed southwards along the Grand Canal. Under the escort of Chinese officials, they began the return trip.

Before leaving, Emperor Zhu Di presented three kings a large number of gifts according to the diplomatic etiquette of giving more and getting less.

The Sulu Voyagers visiting China not only experienced the extensive and profound Chinese culture and strengthened the lateral friendly ties,

在北京的二十七天，苏禄使团目睹了中国的繁荣昌盛，深深感受到中华文明的博大精深，特别对明政府空前的礼遇赞赏有加。永乐十五年（1417 年）八月庚戌日，苏禄东王巴都葛叭答剌、西王麻哈剌叱葛剌麻丁、峒王叭都葛巴剌卜向明成祖及皇太子分别辞行。

对前来告别的苏禄国三位国王，明成祖同样按照"厚往薄来"的外交礼节，赠送给苏禄客人大量的礼品。

明政府对苏禄使团的回赠之物可分为三大种类：一类为象征性的朝服礼器，包括金镶玉带、金绣蟒龙衣、麒麟衣等；一类为真金白银，包括黄金百两，白金二千两，钞一万锭，钱三千贯等；一类为绫罗绸缎，包括罗锦文绮

大明太宗文皇帝實錄

永樂十五年八月庚戌○蘇祿國東王巴都葛叭答剌、西王麻哈剌吒葛剌麻丁、峒王叭都葛巴剌卜辭歸。人賜金鑲玉帶一，黃金百兩，白金二千兩，羅錦文綺二百疋，絹三百疋，鈔一萬錠，錢三千貫，金綉蟒龍衣、麒麟衣各一襲。賜其隨從頭目文綺、綵絹、錢鈔有差。

二百疋，绢三百疋等。除回赠苏禄东、西、峒三王外，属官随从按人头都有不同的文绮、彩绢、钱钞等的赠予。如果加上前者入朝时奉天殿所赐苏禄三王的纱帽、金镶玉带、钑花金带、金蟒龙衣、金银钱钞、珍珠、锦绞丝、纱罗、器皿、铺陈等物，王妃冠服、银钱、纱绞丝等物，王室男女亲戚、头目、使女等人的冠带、衣服等物，明政府所赠之物的实际价值达白银数十万两，而苏禄所贡土特产的价值不过白银万两，明政府所赐之物的价值数十倍于苏禄进贡之物的价值。以上还不包括对苏禄货物的免税部分。这充分显示了明政府对苏禄使团的高度重视和促进两国友好关系的诚意。

苏禄使团此次入华访问，不仅亲身体验了博大精深的中华文化，加强了与中国的友好往来，还实现了多重目的，具有多重意义，取得了良好成效。

政治上，苏禄使团通过访华，与明朝建立正式的宗藩朝贡关系，提高了苏禄在南洋诸国中的政治地位。当时明王朝经济发达、国力强盛、社会文明，许多国家诚心仰慕，南洋、西洋诸国纷纷与中国建立宗藩朝贡关系，这在当时已成为东南亚诸国的政治时尚。苏禄周边的吕宋、冯嘉施兰、古麻剌朗、合猫里等菲律宾群岛上的古国都曾遣使访华或朝贡。在这种情况下，苏禄王不甘落后，也率团入华访问，得到大明王朝的册封与保护，增强自己的国力，巩固了其在菲律宾群岛的国际地位，外交成效显著。

经济上，苏禄使团通过访华，促进了苏禄与中国的贸易往来。苏禄群岛种植业不发达，但水产资源丰富，尤其是盛产珍珠、海龟、海盐等。而中国盛产陶瓷、绫绢、绸缎、布匹、铁器等，是珍珠、香料的最大消费国。因此，苏禄的产业与中国的产业互补性很强，与中国开展商业贸易对两国人民都有利。当时明朝实行的是朝贡贸易，只有与明

and at the same time they were able to achieve the multiple targets, both politically and economically.

Politically, Sulu aimed to establish a formal tributary relation with the Ming government through this visit in order to promote their international status among the Southeast Asian counties. At that time, lots of countries, especially the Southeast Asian countries or regions like Luzon, Pangasinan and Mindanao admired Ming's power and civilization, and were eager to build tributary ties with them. Under such conditions, Sulu was loath to lag behind and adjusted the timely diplomatic strategy. They came to China to pay tribute to the Ming Dynasty and were granted titles of nobility and thereby consolidated their status in Southeast Asia. In a word, they successfully fulfilled their political mission.

Economically, the lateral trade ties were strengthened by their visit to China. Sulu Islands are located near the equator, hot and humid all round year. Coastal cliffs and barren soil are not conducive to planting, but it is rich in the aquatic resources

**The Bridge of Sino-Philippines Friendship**
Marking the 600th Anniversary of the Visit to China by the Sultans of Sulu

奎章

纪念苏禄王访华六百周年

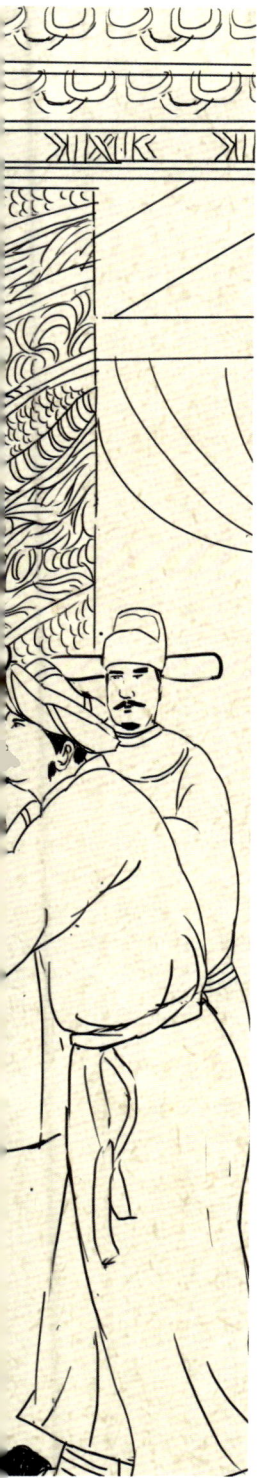

朝确立朝贡关系的国家才能领取明朝颁发的贸易执照签证——勘合，从而取得入华贸易的资格，否则被视为走私。苏禄使团访华后，得到明政府的贸易许可，从而取得入华贸易的合法地位，极大促进了双方贸易的开展。苏禄从中国输入丝绸、瓷器、铁器等物，将珍珠、黄蜡、棉花、玳瑁、木棉和香料等土特产销往中国。中国的丝绸是苏禄人最喜欢的衣料，而瓷器则成为苏禄人生活中不可缺少的物品。苏禄人甚至习惯以拥有瓷器的多少来计算个人的财产，日常生活中的赠予或赔偿也常以中国的瓷器来进行。苏禄出产的珍珠，既大又圆，颜色青白，被称为"极品"，畅销中国内地。苏禄的其他特产如苏木、豆蔻、降香、藤条等也备受中国人的青睐。

社会文化上，随着苏禄与中国政治、经济交往日益密切，从中国传入的牛耕、水车、冶炼、陶瓷制作及织麻等生产技术推动了苏禄国经济社会的发展，文明日益进步。

总之，此次中国之行，苏禄使团顺利地完成了外交使命。他们圆满地结束了对华访问，在中国官员的护送下，按预定的行程，沿京杭大运河南下，踏上了回国的旅程。

Sulu Mission biding farewell to Chinese Emperor (Scenes description)

苏禄国三位国王向明成祖辞行（场景描绘）

with pearls, turtles and sea salt. On the one hand, China was then the biggest consumer of Sulu's specialties like pearls and spices, and on the other hand, Sulu was also dependent on some Chinese products such as porcelain, silk, cloth and iron. Therefore, they complemented each other, thus, forging a friendly relationship that was beneficial to both Sulu and China.

Socially and culturally, the close political and trade ties between Chian and Sulu islands led to the advancement of product technologies and tools from China such as plowing by cow, use of waterwheel, smelting and porcelain making that promoted the social development and progress.

All in all, Sulu Delegation ended their visit to China with an accomplishment of the diplomatic mission and made the return trip along the Grand Canal in accordance with their scheduled route under the escort of Chinese officials.

# Chapter IV
## The Tomb of Paduka Pahala Witnessing Sino-Philippines Friendly Relations

The Sulu mission bid farewell to Emperor Zhu Di and sailed south along the Grand Canal. Paduka Pahala, died of a disease when they got Dezhou town. Emperor Zhu Di felt great sorrow hearing the sad news. He then ordered the officials of Ministry of Rites to write the funeral oration mourning him and ordered the provincial government to hold a kingly ranked funeral for him. Finally, Paduka Pahala was buried in the north of the Dezhou town.

From then on, a 600-year-old tomb has been telling the people a story made by the Silk Road. It stood as a witness in a period of magnificent history by the diplomacy of its chief executives and passing the sustained friendship by the mutual relations and trust.

# 万古流芳

## ——苏禄东王墓成为中菲友好关系的见证

苏禄使团辞别明成祖，沿着运河南下。途经山东德州时，东王巴都葛叭答剌不幸染病逝世。噩耗传到北京，明成祖甚为悲痛，钦命礼部撰写祭文悼念东王，命有司以王礼厚葬这位中菲友好使者于德州城北。

从此，一座长眠六百年的东王墓，讲述着一段因丝绸之路而相遇的故事，书写着一段因元首外交而雄壮的历史，传承着一段因交往互信而持续的情谊。

奎章
纪念苏禄王访华六百周年

# Sulu Sultan Paduka Pahala died of a Disease in Dezhou

## 婴疾遽薨——苏禄东王病逝于中国德州

The Sulu Delegation left Beijing and sailed southwards along the Grand Canal. They passed Tianjin, Jinghai, Cangzhou and Botou and arrived in Dezhou. The local governor heard the news and made preparation for their arrival.

**The Old River Course of Dezhou Grand Canal**
**德州运河故道**

德州地处南运河与卫运河之间，扼京杭大运河之要冲和咽喉，有"九达天衢""神京门户"之称，是当时贯通南北运河的交通枢纽

苏禄使团离京南下，明成祖按王礼派专使护送。苏禄使团一行出齐化门（今朝阳门）至通州，经天津、静海，过沧州、泊头，往德州而来。德州知州闻讯，安排馆驿，做好了迎送苏禄贵宾的准备。

德州官员开驿迎接，却忽闻苏禄东王巴都葛叭答剌突患急症，便将东王安置于德州城北的安陵驿，并寻医诊治。可惜救治无效，永乐十五年（1417年）九月十三日，东王不幸辞世。

苏禄东王所患何病，中外史籍无明确记载。根据明朝疫病情况，东王得的很可能是中国北方秋季极易流行的一种"秋瘟"（参见夏春江《苏禄国王和苏禄国王墓》，中国

大明太宗文皇帝實錄

永樂十五年九月乙丑○蘇祿國東王巴都葛叭答剌歸次德州，病卒，訃聞。遣官賜祭，命有司營墳，葬以王禮。

海洋大学出版社 2002 年版），也可能得的是疟疾。由于古代医疗条件有限，恶性疟疾感染者一旦患病，短时间内便可致死。东王回国时，正值华北地区疟疾高发的时节，加上旅途劳顿，人很容易染病。苏禄东王可能过沧州不久便染上恶性疟疾，发病后昏迷不醒，因当时并无医治此病的良药，因而很快病逝。

苏禄东王病逝时的年龄，史籍也无记载。当时苏禄东王携王妃及三子入华，三位王子的年龄虽无记载，但王长子都麻含在苏禄东王病逝后袭王爵率众南归，独立行使王权，可见当时他已成人。王次子安都鲁、王三子温哈剌留华守墓并客居中国，他们的妻子分别为息剌安、嗒剌一林，都是苏禄女子，由此可推知王子安都鲁、温哈剌来华时也已长大成人，并可能已婚。如此看来，苏禄东王的年纪应不小于四十岁。而从祾恩殿供奉的苏禄东王画像推知，其年龄也不会超过五十岁。因而苏禄东王病逝时应在四十至五十岁之间。

苏禄东王突然病逝，使苏禄使团不得不改变原定行程，暂停于德州馆驿。随行的明政府官员一面安抚东王眷属，一面急报入京。

苏禄东王病逝于德州的消息传到北京，明成祖不胜痛悼，敕谕安慰随行眷属，即派礼部郎中陈士启携《谕祭文》赶赴德州，祭奠东王。

Everything was ready, but word came that Sulu Sultan Paduka Pahala got an acute disease. Unfortunately, he died on the 13th of September, 1417 A.D..

The sudden death of Paduka Pahala delayed the schedule of the Sulu mission as they decided to stay in Dezhou. The accompanying Chinese officials gave his relatives a place to stay for the meantime as they sent the news to Beijing as quickly as possible.

Upon hearing the grievous news, Emperor Yongle was so sorrowful that he expressed his condolences to the bereaved family on the death of the king, and sent Chen Shiqi, an official in the Ministry of Rites, to Dezhou with the funeral oration.

**The Bridge of Sino-Philippines Friendship**
Marking the 600th Anniversary of the Visit to China by the Sultans of Sulu

奎章
纪念苏禄王访华六百周年

# The Chinese Emperor Held a Grand Funeral for Sulu Sultan Paduka Pahala

## 垂于无极——中国皇帝厚葬苏禄东王

According to the Chinese royal funeral standard, Paduka Pahala was buried in the southwest of the Twelve Barracks, north of Dezhou with a gravestone beside the tomb in memory of him.

Dezhou was then a well-known canal town. Being the traffic artery, the city was the only way to Beijing either by land or by water from south provinces of China, so it got the reputation as the "Junction of Nine Arteries". The reason why Emperor Zhu Di chose this vital traffic hub with beautiful scenery as East King's burying place was because he wanted to express admiration for Paduka Pahala, and on the other hand, he intended to let the later generations remember thepioneer of the Sino-Sulu friendship forever.

为了表达对苏禄东王的哀悼，明成祖特命按照亲王的礼制，在德州城北的"十二连城"西南营墓立碑。

当时德州不仅是运河名城，而且地处南北交通要道，是南方各省进京的水陆路必经之地，素有"九达天衢"之称。德州运河河段内"舳舻相冲，千里不绝，官艘贾舶，联翔方载"，商船"南逾苏杭，远浮翯广，北越京津"，城内"大聚四方之俗，探奇货于游市，号为百商之渊"。墓址选于德州城北，一是该处"一城拱卫环绕，风水所聚"。王墓背有十二连城拱卫，前有护城河，正应风水所言"依山面水"之宝地。二是王墓西临运河，风景宜人。明成祖择此水陆要冲、景色秀美之地营葬东王，除了表达对其"诚贯金石"的敬佩之外，也是为了让后人永远铭记这位中菲友好的使者。

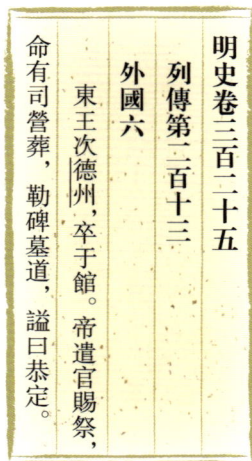

明史卷三百二十五
列传第二百十三
外國六
東王次德州，卒于館。帝遣官賜祭，命有司營葬，勒碑墓道，謚曰恭定。

Map of Tomb of Puduka Pahala, Ming Dynasty
明代德州苏禄东王墓位置示意图

《温安家乘要录·陵墓》载：德州城北二里许，土垒十二所，周方数里，绵亘连峙，旧名十二连城。系前明建文时李景隆将兵屯驻之地。王薨，卜葬于其西南隅。一城拱卫环绕，风水所聚

永乐十五年（1417年）十月三日，礼部郎中陈士启，宣读御制祭文，为东王举行了隆重的安葬仪式。

在祭文中，明成祖高度赞誉苏禄东王"聪慧明达，赋性温厚"，肯定了东王访华对两国友好关系所做出的杰出贡献，盛赞东王的事迹"昭播后世，与天地相为悠久"，对东王的不幸逝世表达了"不胜痛悼"之情。明成祖还按照帝王将相死后赠谥的惯例，赐赠东王谥号"恭定"。"恭定"有恭敬、谦逊之意，是对明君、贤王死后的褒奖。以此号赐赠苏禄东王，表达了永乐皇帝对苏禄东王的钦佩与敬仰。

On the 3rd day of October, the 15th year of Emperor Yongle's reign (11th of September 1417 A.D.), a magnificent funeral ceremony was held with Chen Shiqi, an Official of the Ministry of Rites, giving the elegiac address.

*The Funeral Oration* Written by the Yongle Emperor

明成祖《谕祭文》

惟王聰慧明達，賦性溫厚，敬天之道，誠事知幾，不憚數萬里，率其眷屬及陪臣、國人，歷涉海道，忠順之心，可謂至矣。茲特厚加賞賚，錫以恩誥，封以王爵，俾爾身家榮顯，福爾一國之人。近命還國，何其嬰疾，遽焉殞逝，訃音來聞，不勝痛悼！今特賜爾諡曰恭定，仍命爾子承爾王爵，率其眷屬回還。於戲！死生者人理之常，於爾享爵祿於生前，垂福慶於後嗣，身雖死歿，而賢德令名昭播後世，與天地相爲悠久，雖死猶生，復何憾焉。茲用遣人祭以牲醴，九泉有知，尚克享之！

东王安葬后，明成祖仍余悲未尽，又于永乐十六年（1418 年）敕令在苏禄东王墓前修建祠庙，立碑纪念，并亲书碑文，即现存的"御制苏禄国东王碑"，永垂后世。碑文字里行间流露出对苏禄东王的钦佩与敬重，以及对东王逝世的惋惜与哀悼，指出"今王慕义而来，诚贯金石，不谓婴疾，遽殒厥身，其忠义不可泯，故用纪其实，以诏后世"。盛赞东王"聪明特达，超出等伦"，高度评价

Chen Shiqi, an Official of Ministry of Rites, Appointed by Emperor Holding the Funeral Ceremony for Puduka Pahala (Scenes description)

礼部郎中陈士启主持安葬仪式（场景描绘）

东王使华的功绩是"光荣被其家国，庆泽流于后人，名声昭于史册，永世而不磨"。碑文最后赞曰："王虽薨逝，盖有不随死而亡者，此诚大丈夫矣。"

为了让后人看到苏禄东王之容颜，明成祖还特命宫中

The funeral oration spoke highly of Paduka Pahala, affirmed his visit to China as an outstanding contribution to the friendship between two countries, and declared his deeds would be remembered for as long as the heaven and earth exist. According to Chinese traditional royal customs, he was conferred the posthumous title Gongding that means high respect and modesty.

Ancient City on the Grand Canal and the Tomb of Puduka Pahala

运河古城及苏禄东王墓图（王宪贞绘制）

Emperor Yongle still felt grieved for the East King even after his funeral, and next year he issued the imperial order of building temples in front of the tomb and wrote the inscriptions personally carved in the gravestone.

画师绘制了一幅苏禄东王肖像，悬挂于陵墓的享殿中央，以供后人瞻仰。

苏禄东王是大明王朝御赐国王，故明成祖"命有司营坟，葬以王礼"。陵墓的建造，先墓后庙，从建宝顶开始至享殿建成，前后经过近一年的时间。永乐十六年（1418年）九月，苏禄国王陵墓修建完成。

**Tablet Made by Emperor Order for Puduka Pahala**

**御制苏禄国东王碑**

御制苏禄国东王碑通高2.475米，阔1.075米，上有螭首，下有龟趺

## Rubbings of Puduka Pahala Tablet
## 《御制苏禄国东王碑》拓片

碑额篆刻有碑名——御制苏禄国东王碑，中部镌刻阴文楷书碑文。历经近六个世纪的风风雨雨，字迹仍苍劲有力，清晰可辨

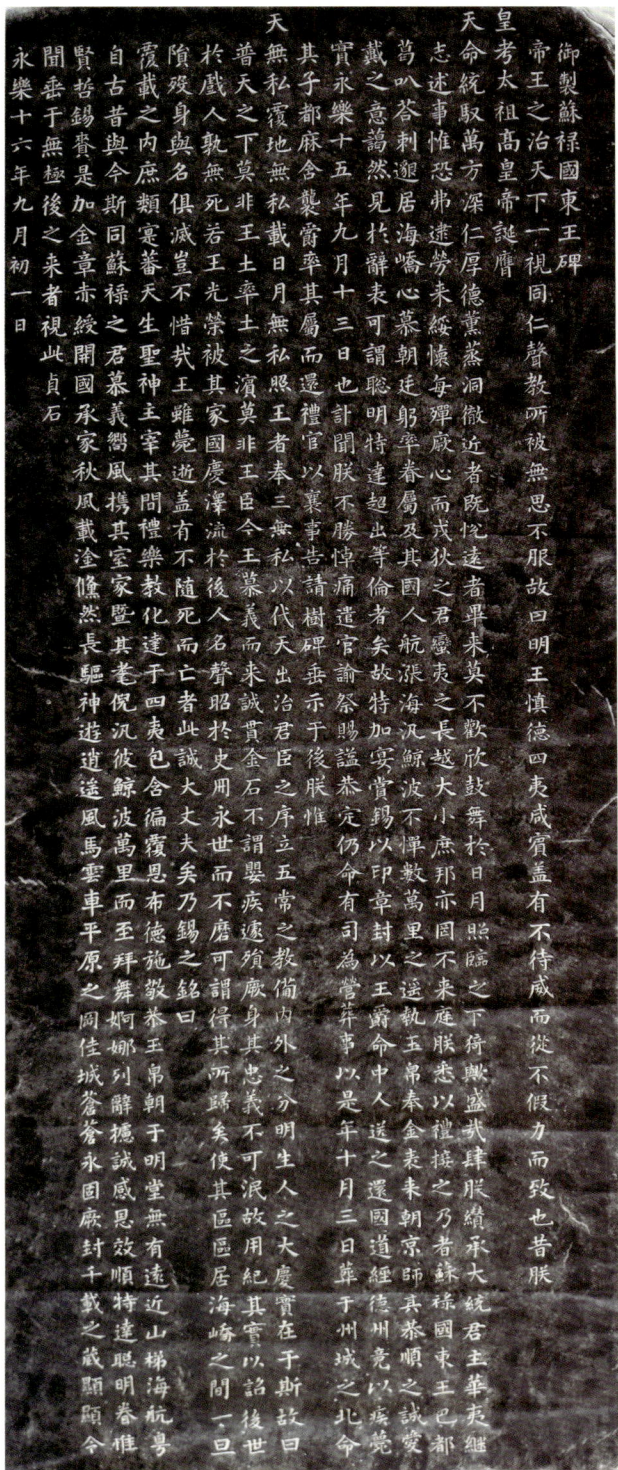

御製蘇祿國東王碑

皇考太祖高皇帝誕膺
天命統馭萬方深仁厚德薰蒸洞微

志述事惟恐弗逮勞來綏懷每殫厥心而戎狄之君靈夷之長越大小庶邦罔不來庭悉以禮接之乃昔蘇祿國東王巳都
葛叭谷利邇居海嶠心慕朝廷及其國人航涉海汎鯨波不憚萬里之遙執玉帛奉金表來朝京師其恭順之誠愛
戴之意藹然見於辭來可謂聰明特達超出等倫者矣故特加宴賞錫以印章封以王爵命中人送之還國道經德州薨以疾薨
實永樂十五年九月十三日也計聞朕不勝悼痛遣官諭祭賜以命有司為營葬事以是年十月三日葬于州城之北命

天無私覆地無私載日月無私照莫非王土率土之濱莫非王臣朕奉三無私以代天出治君臣之序立五常之教備內外之分明生人之大慶實在于斯故曰
普天之下莫非王土率土之濱莫非王臣而不磨可謂得其所歸矣使其區區居海嶠之間一旦
於戲人執無死王雖薨逝蓋有不隨死而亡者此誠大丈夫乃錫之銘曰
隕歿身與名俱滅堂不惜我王雖薨逝蓋有不隨死而亡者此誠大丈夫乃錫之銘曰
其子都麻含嚳率其屬而還禮官以襄事告請樹碑垂示於後朕惟

帝王之治天下一視同仁聲教所被無思不服故曰明王慎德四夷咸賓蓋有不待威而從不假力而致也昔朕

覆載之內庶類同蘇祿之君與今
自古昔與今蘇祿之君慕義嚮風携其室家暨其卷倪汎彼鯨波萬里而至拜舞闕庭誠感恩效順特達聰明眷惟近山梯海航粤
賢哲垂錫賚是加金章赤綬開國承家秋風戴淦儼然長驅神遊逍遰風馬雲車平原之岡佳城蒼蒼永固廠封千載之載顯顯令
聞垂于無極後之來者視此貞石
永樂十六年九月初一日

**The Bridge of Sino-Philippines Friendship**
Marking the 600th Anniversary of the Visit to China by the Sultans of Sulu

奎章

纪念苏禄王访华六百周年

Image of Puduka Pahala (Offered by Dezhou Sulu Culture Museum)

苏禄东王肖像（德州苏禄文化博物馆提供）

原东王画像绘制于永乐十六年（1418年），后由东王后裔保管。抗日战争时，日寇占领德州期间，东王画像被日寇搜出并遗弃，头部以上部位损毁，后被东王后裔温守龄发现，取回藏于家中，直至1957年送山东省博物馆收藏。现东王画像系2007年以山东省博物馆珍藏的原苏禄国王画像为蓝本，采用国宝金丝贴工艺重新制作而成

In order to let the future generations see what Paduka Pahala looked like, Emperor Yongle commanded specially the palace painter to paint a portrait for him, which was enshrined in the temple and worshiped by the people.

In September, 1418 A.D., the tomb was completed and it took nearly one year.

The Tomb faces south with a temple in front. There built memorial archway, royal Pailou, sacred path, sacrifice hall and tomb from south to north in turn. The memorial tablet of Paduka Pahala is placed in the royal

纵观苏禄东王墓，坐北朝南，"前庙后墓，魂魄相依"。自南而北依次为牌坊、御碑楼、神道、享殿、王墓。其中，御碑楼内存放御制苏禄国东王碑；神道南首东西各立华表一对，沿神道两侧摆放石像生若干种类、若干对；享殿为四合院式建筑布局，正前方为正殿——祾恩殿，前后五楹，殿正中供奉东王画像；王墓封土为圆式宝顶，冢丘的高度

为全德州城最高，地方官吏、缙绅、百姓均不得超越。东王墓前曾立墓碑一方，为安葬仪式结束后的当日所立，上书"故苏禄国恭定王墓"，落款为"大明永乐十五年十月初三日立"，此墓碑至今仍完好陈列于西配殿内。

Pailou. The sacred path is lined with the stone figures and with two pairs of huabiao（engraved pillar in front of a palace, tomb）in the south. The building layout of the sacrifice hall is a quadrangle, in front of which is the main palace, named Ling'en Palace where the portrait of the East King is hanged. According the emperor's order, the tomb was built with a round dome, and any tomb built later in the town must not be higher than it. In front of the tomb stood a memorial gravestone, which was erected on the burial day. It still remains intact and is displayed in the west wing room.

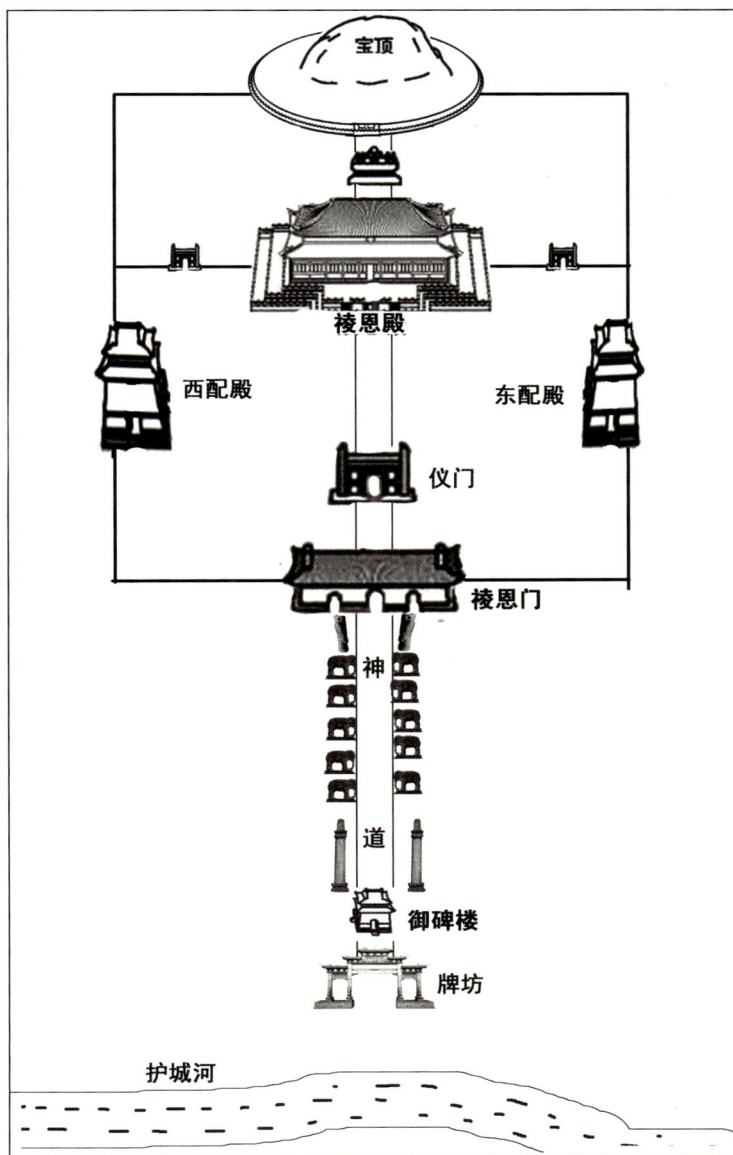

宝顶

棱恩殿

西配殿　　　东配殿

仪门

棱恩门

神

道

御碑楼

牌坊

护城河

**Drawing of Puduka Pahala Tomb, Ming Dynasty**
明代苏禄东王墓形制图

根据明朝陵寝制度，王陵一般形制为前殿后墓、坐北向南；自前往后一般为牌坊、神道碑、华表、石像生、享殿、宝顶等。东王墓即按此形制建造

**The Bridge of Sino-Philippines Friendship**
Marking the 600th Anniversary of the Visit to China by the Sultans of Sulu

奎章

纪念苏禄王访华六百周年

# The Chinese Government Repairs the Tomb of Paduka Pahala

## 丰碑永存——中国政府修葺苏禄东王墓

Sulu Sultans' visit to China was regarded as a grand event in the history of Sino-Philippines relationship and the Sulu King's tomb is the best witness. In the past 600 years, the successive Chinese feudal governments and Chinese people have been taking care of it seriously, and some maintenance work has been done many times.

After the tomb was built, Ming government took lots of measures to ensure that it was preserved well. During Wanli period, given the Sulu's religious belief, a mosque was built beside the tomb.

苏禄三王率使团访华是中菲友好交往史上的一件盛事。位于中国山东德州的苏禄东王陵墓是中菲友好交往的历史见证。六百年来，中国历代政府和百姓重视苏禄东王陵墓的保护，多次对其进行修葺。

苏禄东王陵墓建成后，明政府对王墓很重视，加之东王后裔精心看护，王墓得到妥善保护。万历年间，明政府考虑到苏禄王及其后裔的宗教信仰，特赐在东王墓旁建造一座清真寺，以便以伊斯兰教仪式祭奠苏禄东王。

明清鼎革之际，社会长期战乱，王墓逐渐荒废。至清康熙年间，"太息松楸尽，牛羊上墓阡"，杂草丛生，满目荒凉。清雍正十一年（1733年），苏禄国王母汉末母拉律林遣使访华，上表雍正皇帝，请求修葺其先祖东王巴都葛叭答剌在山东德州的坟墓，赒恤留居中国看守王墓的东王子孙。雍正随即敕令礼部负责对东王墓进行勘查、整饬、修葺，并封东王后裔二人为"奉祀生"，赐予顶戴，负责王墓的维护与祭奠。

由于日久年深、风雨侵蚀，至清末民初，苏禄东王陵墓再次毁损严重，"殿宇倾圮"。尤其是1927年，恩县耿李庄运河东决，给墓地造成极大的破坏。当时，德州城"水绕城垣，仅露七砖"。德州城外一片汪洋，大水淹没神道，王墓仅露墓顶。大水过后，御碑被大水冲陷于泥中，翁仲石马东倒西歪。东王后裔变卖枯树，劝募捐款，筹集资金，重筑高台，对王墓和御碑做了必要修整。

20世纪40年代，东王第十五代孙安树德自天津回乡，看到东王墓为水灾和战火所毁，满目疮痍，痛心万分，便捐款捐物，对东王墓、清真寺、碑亭等进行修葺。他将自己珍藏的国宝——"祭红宝瓶"捐献给清真寺，安置于清真寺礼拜大殿的殿脊顶部，成为清真寺最亮丽的一景。

1949年新中国成立后，中国政府十分重视保护苏禄国王墓。1956年，苏禄国东王墓被列为山东省文物保护单位；1977年被列为山东省第一批重点文物保护单位；1988年国务院公布德州苏禄国东王墓为全国重点文物保护单位。从1965年至今，中国各级政府先后十余次拨款，陆续对苏禄国王墓进行扩建、修葺，逐步形成如今庄严肃穆、古朴典雅的王墓建筑群——苏禄东王墓园。

In 1733 A.D. (11<sup>th</sup> year of Emperor Yongzheng's Period), Sulu Sultan's mother Nasirudin dispatched the envoy to China. As soon as the delegation arrived in Beijing, her letter was submitted to Yongzheng's Period, in which she not only expressed her gratitude to Ming government, but also put forward a request of renovating Paduka Pahala's tomb and resuming the pension given to his offspring in China. The Chinese government did as the request.

**Unrepaired Puduka Pahala Tomb** (about early 1950s)
复建前的苏禄东王墓
（新中国成立初期拍摄）

奎章

纪念苏禄王访华六百周年

今日之苏禄东王墓园位于中国山东省德州市区西北部，过北陵桥北行便是通向墓园的主道——北陵路。路口耸立着高大的石牌坊，上镌"苏禄王御园"五个镏金大字。牌坊结构为四楹三间，石额正反两面均以浅浮雕手法镌刻二龙戏珠图案，龙形逼真，雕技精湛，似跃水而出，扶摇穿云而上。柱基四面为浅浮雕二狮戏球，活灵活现。四柱前后，各有两只石狮守护，仪态威严。

穿过石牌坊，沿幽雅的青砖路北行约一百米，路中屹立一座朱漆四角方亭，上书"御碑亭"。亭顶为单层檐歇

**Stone  Memorial Archway**

石牌坊

**Imperial Stele Pavilion**
御碑亭

In 1940s, An Shude (the 15th gene-ration grandson of Paduka Pahala) came back home from Tianjin. He repaired the tomb and donated the priceless bottle he collected to the mosque, which was placed on the top of the dome of the mosque.

After the People's Republic of China was established, the Chinese government have been paying much attention to the protection for the Sulu Sultan's tomb. In 1956, the Sulu Sultan's tomb was listed in the provincial cultural relics and in 1977, it upgraded to the first key cultural relics of Shandong Province. In 1988, it became the national key cultural relic. Since 1965, the financial grant from the state has been given to it tens of times for its repair and extension. Nowadays a solemn classical refined cemetery has come into being.

山式，黄色琉璃瓦，四角飞檐，飞檐上有羽化仙人和各种瑞兽，檐下雕梁画栋，工艺极其细腻。亭内陈列着高大的石碑，上有螭首，下有龟趺。碑额刻"御制苏禄国东王碑"，中部镌刻阴文楷书碑文。此碑为复制品，真品陈放于御碑楼内。

从御碑亭往北行约二百米，路中间是神道牌楼。牌楼系三洞门，中门宽四米，边门各宽一点五米，中高侧低，

**Decorated Archway on the Tomb Passage**

神道牌楼

四根红色方柱坐落在约一米见方的基座上；上部雕梁画栋，歇山挑檐，黄琉璃瓦盖顶。门楣正面系中国书法家协会前主席启功先生书写的"芳名远播"，门楣背面系上海书画院谢稚柳先生书写的"聪慧永传"。

牌楼东侧约三十米处为御碑楼，此楼系 20 世纪 40 年代苏禄东王后裔安树德所建。楼内陈放永乐十六年（1418年）所立的"御制苏禄国东王碑"真品。

神道牌楼以北是长约一百米的神道，石像生分列两侧，现仅存狮、虎、羊、马四对。神道南端是一对石狮，头上鬃毛卷曲，胸前的火云纹和前肢的鬃毛如随风飘荡，再加上昂首怒目的姿态，更显得威武不凡。石狮北侧为华表一对，华表柱头是圆雕的摩尼珠，摩尼珠呈胡桃形，柱身呈八棱形，每个棱面都刻有精致的蔓草海石榴花纹。华表以北为石虎一对，仰面、张吻、扣齿，暴目圆睁，鼻部显得突出，大鼻唇，鼻孔上豁，双耳直竖，颈下部及前腿上部刻火焰纹，背部正中脊骨突起，周身为小圆型凸起云纹，尾粗而短，前后腿内侧刻成凹棱状，使该兽显得矫健、凶猛。石虎以北为石羊，羊呈卧状，昂首平视，两只羊角卷至耳下，体态匀称，神情温顺。石羊以北为石马，嘴微张露齿，

The Building Which Used to Protect the Imperial Stele

御碑楼

# The Bridge of Sino-Philippines Friendship
### Marking the 600th Anniversary of the Visit to China by the Sultans of Sulu

奎章

纪念苏禄王访华六百周年

## Tomb Passage
神道

## Stone Figures beside the Tomb Passage（Stone Figures of Civil and Military Officials  Stone Lion, Stone Horse and Officers in Charge of Horses）

神道石像（翁仲、石狮、石马及控马官）

双目圆睁，双耳直竖，略带惊疑神色，笼头、鞍辔、带饰等一应俱全，且雕刻手法十分现实、逼真、细腻，胸前挂饰有缨无铃，鞍垫纹饰细腻，以桃叶图案为主，马鞍上部精雕花卉图案，下部为圆形云龙图案。马的旁边为两尊控马官，东侧控马官为武将，头戴盔、身披甲；西侧控马官为文官，头戴素纹官帽，腰间系镶玉腰带。最后为两尊翁仲，是石刻仪仗中最高者，在整个石刻群中显得高大突出。翁仲属文官，双手自然合于胸前，怀抱笏板，双目俯视神道中央，一副恭侍王驾的神态。

神道北端便是陵墓主体建筑——四合院式的享殿。正中为祾恩门，即享殿大门。祾恩门共三间，宽十米，进深五点五米，琉璃瓦盖顶，为木制朱红色大门。从祾恩门进入，正前方约三十米为祾恩殿，有青石甬道相通，左右两侧分别为西配殿、东配殿，四周以廊庑连通。沿青石甬道而行，

Today's Sulu cemetery has become an ancient architectural complex, composed of the tomb, sacrifice hall, pailou, memorial archway, sacred path and mosque. The whole buildings are in the graceful order and creates a new style. The solemn tomb is surrounded by the pines and cypress trees. On the entrance of the sacred path stands a white marble pailou, which is lined with the stone pillars and stone human and animal statues. The tombs of Kamulin, Wen Hala and An Dulu are located in the southeast side of Paduka Pahalas'. The mosque lies in the west side of Ling'en Palace, which has become the place for the religious service.

东侧为 1988 年所立"全国重点文物保护单位"石碑一座，甬道正中大理石基座上嵌碑两方，一方是 1999 年菲律宾社团与苏禄苏丹联合捐献的英文铁碑——苏禄国王墓纪念碑；一方由德州市政府将英文碑用中文重新镌刻在汉白玉石上，镶嵌在英文铁碑之侧。庄严肃穆的祾恩殿建在一米高的砖石基座上，五脊出檐，绿色琉璃瓦盖顶，东西跨度十八米多，南北进深七米多，斗拱昂枋，前后装红色木制棂门。殿前是八根朱漆立柱支撑的前廊，中间两柱篆刻对联一副：上联为"层云渺渺魂南望"，下联配"细雨潇潇水北流"。此联深刻反映了苏禄东王南望故国，北仰京城，希望中菲世代友好的良好愿望。殿内正中供奉苏禄国东王画像，画像两侧立柱上篆刻金字楹联，上联为"梯山航海朝丹阙，赤绶金章拜凤楼"，下联为"生寄百蛮居化外，

**Ling'en Gate**
祾恩门

Ling'en Palace
祾恩殿

Imperial Tomb
王墓冢

死归万里葬荒丘"。殿前东西两侧是配殿，筒瓦椽门。大门、正殿、配殿之间有长廊连接，红柱灰瓦，画栋粉墙。

祾恩殿以北是高大的王墓宝顶，高台上苍松翠柏，台下国槐成荫，整个墓地郁郁葱葱，绿草如茵。中国全国人大常委会原副委员长费孝通和外交部原副部长齐怀远观瞻后，分别题词："东亚一家，友谊长存"，"中菲友好，源远流长"。如今墓冢松涛声声，殿宇熠熠生辉，异域国王长眠

Aerial Photo of Puduka Pahala Tomb
苏禄东王墓航拍图

于此，正如永乐皇帝祭文所说："享爵禄于生前，垂福庆于后嗣，身虽死殁，而贤德令名昭播后世，与天地相为悠久，虽死犹生，复何憾焉。"

从祾恩殿出来，在祾恩门东侧约五十米处是王妃葛木宁与二位王子安都鲁、温哈剌墓。三墓相依，与东王墓相望。

在祾恩门西侧为清真寺。该座清真寺历经多次修葺，成为以苏禄东王后裔为主体的穆斯林群众举行礼拜和祭奠苏禄东王的场所。清真寺坐西朝东，三开式朱漆大门、斗拱飞檐、红柱金瓦。走进大门，南北经堂分列两侧，呈对称布局。礼拜堂处于整个清真寺建筑群的中轴线上，为长方形砖木殿宇式建筑，由前殿、中殿和后窑殿三部分组成，雕梁画栋，绿琉璃瓦盖顶，古朴典雅，庄严肃穆。

## Mosque Gate
清真寺大门

## Religious Service Hall in Mosque
清真寺礼拜堂

15世纪之初的苏禄国笃信伊斯兰教,于是守墓人带着他们的信仰生活于德州时,清真寺便成为必不可少的心系之所。寺内还设有"苏禄东王在华后裔通谱编委会",可见在宗教功能之外,清真寺还充当了联结苏禄东王后裔的纽带

奎章
纪念苏禄王访华十六百周年

**The Bridge of Sino-Philippines Friendship**
Marking the 600th Anniversary of the Visit to China by the Sultans of Sulu

# The Chinese Government Holds a Memorial Ceremony for East King Sulu Sultan Paduka Pahala

## 世代缅怀——中国政府祭奠苏禄东王

As the goodwill envoy between China and the Philippines, Paduka Pahala has been venerated by the Chinese governments of the different periods and its people. The people of the two countries have been holding the memorial ceremony for him since then.

After the funeral, Emperor Zhu Di allowed Paduka Pahala's wife and his two sons to stay in China as grave keepers for three years according to the Chinese custom. At the same time, Chen Yaozhu, Ma Chousi and Xia Naima and their family who were Muslims inhabitants of Licheng county were ordered to migrate to Dezhou to serve Sulu guests. The memorial ceremony and Ghost Festival are held in Qingming Festival every year. During Wanli period of the Ming Dynasty, the mosque was built and Ming government never ceased to hold the memorial ceremony since Emperor Yongle reigned. The Ahung and the

苏禄东王作为中菲友谊的使者，受到中国历代政府的重视和人民的敬仰。中菲人民对苏禄东王墓的祭奠以及对苏禄东王的缅怀悼念活动，一直延续至今。

安葬苏禄东王后，为表示对他的哀悼，明成祖特意按照中国风俗，准许东王妃、二位王子及随从在中国守墓三年，并拨历城县（今济南历下区）回民陈咬柱、马丑斯、夏乃马三户"永远相兼看守王墓，供给王裔役使，耕种祭田，供王祀事"；特设春、秋二祭，每逢春季清明、秋季中元节举行祭祀东王的活动。永乐以后，明政府对苏禄东王墓的祭奠活动一直没有中断。万历年间，清真寺建成后，每逢回教大典，清真寺的阿訇还会率东王后裔诵经祭墓。

清政府对苏禄东王墓的祭奠始于雍正年间。当时，一度中断的中国与苏禄的政治联系得到恢复，清政府对东王的祭祀活动也随之开始。雍正十一年（1733年），雍正皇帝封东王后裔中的二人为"奉祀生"，同时设春、秋二祭。此后，每逢春季清明、秋季中元，德州知州都要乘轿亲赴东王墓，举行隆重的祭奠仪式，代表朝廷宣读祭文。

为了保障春、秋二祭的举行，清政府还制定了《清朝谕祭典册》，对春、秋二祭的承办事宜做出具体详细的规定。可见，清政府对苏禄东王墓的祭奠已经制度化，即使乾隆二十八年（1763年）后中国和苏禄政府间的往来中断，对东王的祭祀活动也未因此而中止。

The Funeral Orations written by Emperor Order at Qingming Festival and Ghost Festival, Qing Dynasty
清朝历年春季清明、秋季中元节谕祭文

諭祭文

維某年歲次某，某月某日，山東濟南府德州知州某等，遵承禮部札付，欽奉皇帝聖旨，諭祭于蘇祿國恭定王巴都葛叭答剌曰：惟王聰明特達，輸誠慕義，歸向朝廷，生享榮名，歿承褒寵。今因春〈秋〉一季，謹以牲醴，用申詞〈嘗〉祭。神其不昧，來格來歆。尚饗！

## 清朝谕祭典册

为祭祀以肃大典事，今将城北苏禄国恭定东王春秋二季祭祀事宜定例，逐一开列于后。须至册者。

计开：

主王祖先前祭祀等物。

主祭官酒席，以及礼宾、承祭、王孙酒席。

以上系坟夫夏户备办。

桌椅、围屏、净水盆巾、祭酒炭等物。

以上系坟夫马户伺候。

火花果树彩红着酒行人奉节，祖堂添土，修筑人段。

以上系坟户陈户经管伺候料理。

修理垣墙。

夏户管柒拾堵，陈户管拾堵，马户管贰拾堵。

苏禄王后裔姓名：

长支温哈剌后：温明梁、温明桥、温明瑞、温崇辉、温九富等。

次支安都鲁后：安国龙、安瑞符等。

三户：

马祷思，即祥瑞；

夏乃，即如方；

陈瑶生，即士琦。

descendants of Paduka Pahala would chant the Koran on with a grand Muslim ceremony.

From the period of Emperor Yongzheng's reign, Qing government began to hold the memorial ceremony for Paduka Pahala. In 1733 AD. (11th year of Emperor Yongzheng's Period), Emperor Yongzheng conferred two members of Paduka Pahala's descendants the title of Xiucai. Every Qingming and Ghost Festival, the governor of Dezhou would hold the grand memorial ceremony and read the elegiac address on behalf of the court. Qing government even laid down the law to ensure the memorial ceremony to be held in spring and autumn.

纪念苏禄王访华六百周年

### Descendants of Puduka Pahala holding the Memorial Ceremony

### 祭祀大典

东王墓前，十多位长者唱诵经文，祈祷国泰民安，家族兴旺。随后，他们在墓冢边绕走，一一拜祭。这是一次寻常的祭礼。这样的祭礼，人少时三三两两，人多时可上千。不变的是，它日复一日，上演了整整六百个春秋

During the Republic of China, some officials paid the worshipful visit to the tomb of Paduka Pahala together, and later the nonscheduled visits emerged constantly. Taking into consideration civil protection and memorial activities still went on.

Every 13th of September which is the day of Paduka Pahala's death, his descendants held the memorial ceremony in front of the tomb, chanting Koran together with Ahung.

民国虽为乱世，但对苏禄东王墓的祭奠却延续了下来。民国元年（1912年），德县（今德州）县长乘坐四人抬的大轿，打着旗、锣、伞、扇，吹着长号，到东王墓前祭扫，由东王后裔文秀才温如盘、武秀才安福海作陪，摆设供席，搭设临时席棚，并有十余士兵保卫。这是中国政府官员最后一次乘轿致祭。不过一直到1923年，德县县长、官员还集体祭拜过苏禄东王墓，以后仍有各级政府官员不定期地到东王墓凭吊、祭扫。

民国时期，民间对王墓的保护和祭扫活动也在继续。20世纪40年代，原西北军将领、东王第十五代孙安树德解甲还乡后，捐款捐物，并率全村穆斯林对东王墓进行定期祭扫。

如今，每年9月13日苏禄王祭日，苏禄东王后裔就会齐聚于东王墓前，按伊斯兰教习俗，由阿訇率后裔们诵读《古兰经》，举行祭祀大典。

# The Chinese' Best Minds Visit the Tomb of Paduka Pahala

## 凭吊抒怀——中国文人墨客拜谒苏禄东王墓

苏禄东王墓建成后，中国的许多文人墨客都曾驻足拜谒，凭吊这位异国君王，颂扬他"航涨海、泛鲸波，不惮数万里之遥"来华访问，以情深意切的诗歌来寄托对逝者的缅怀与哀思。这些凭吊苏禄国王墓的佳作传世，表达了中国文人儒士对苏禄东王的钦佩之情，为苏禄东王墓留下了一笔可贵的文学遗产。

A lot of literary writers came to pay the respectful visit to Paduka Pahala's tomb with poems in memory of him and in praise of his great deed which have been the precious cultural inheritance.

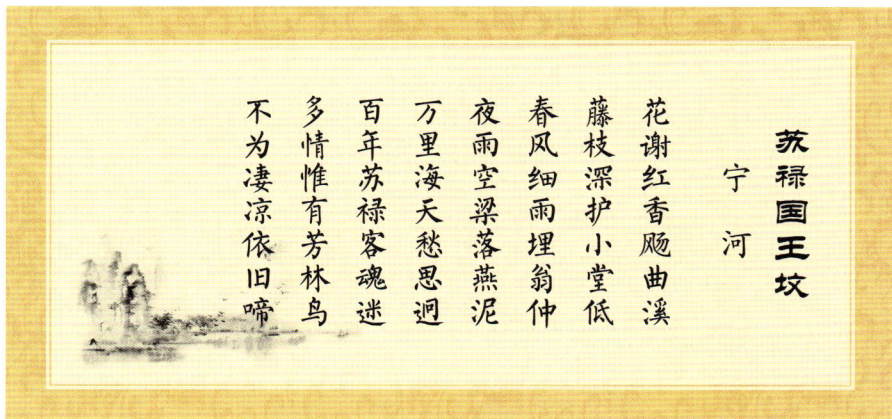

苏禄国王坟
宁河

花谢红香飓曲溪
藤枝深护小堂低
春风细雨埋翁仲
夜雨空梁落燕泥
万里海天愁思迥
百年苏禄客魂迷
多情惟有芳林鸟
不为凄凉依旧啼

宁河，字通州，明代人，曾任德州知州。他在"春风细雨""花谢红香"之时，作七律《苏禄国王坟》一首，凭吊苏禄东王墓。孤寂的王墓在浓浓春意的强烈反衬下，更显凄楚，引起了宁河对这位客逝异国的君王的哀思；"多情惟有芳林鸟，不为凄凉依旧啼"，寄寓着他对苏禄东王诚挚的忆念。

## 过苏禄国王墓

顾炎武

永乐十五年九月，苏禄国东王来朝，归次德州，病卒。遣官赐祭，命有司营坟，上亲为文，树碑墓道，留其侍从十人守墓，其后子孙依而居焉。余过之，出祝版一通，乃嘉靖年者，宛然如故，其字体今人亦不能及矣。

丰碑遥见炳奎题
尚忆先朝宠日碑
世有国人供洒扫
每勤词客驻轮蹄
九河冰壮龙孤出
十二城荒白鹤栖
下马一为邻子问
中原云鸟正凄迷

顾炎武，字宁人，号亭林，明清之际中国著名思想家、学者、诗人。明亡以后，他于1656年只身北上，辗转于山东、河北、山西、陕西一带，其间途经德州，驻足苏禄东王墓前，凭吊古人，有感而发，作七律《过苏禄国王墓》。在诗中，他追忆苏禄东王在明代生前死后所受的礼遇，明代时王墓"世有国人供洒扫"，而今因为战乱，却是"十二城荒白鹤栖"的荒凉景象，表达了顾炎武对苏禄东王及明王朝的无限哀思。

苏禄国王墓

王士禛

当年重译入长安　属国威仪尽汉官

万里沧波归路远　九河春雨墓门寒

空闻蝼蚁生金粟　无复鱼膏照玉棺

欲荐溪毛重回首　乱鸦残日夕漫漫

　　王士禛，字子真，别号渔洋山人，清初中国著名学者，官至刑部尚书。善文辞，尤工诗，主文坛数十年。王士禛途经德州，瞻仰苏禄东王墓，作七律《苏禄国王墓》，缅怀当年苏禄东王不远万里来华，受到隆重的接待，感喟东王不幸客逝中国。而今面对因战乱而荒废的王陵，他愁思万千，寄托着深深的哀思，表达了对苏禄东王的敬仰之情。

苏禄国王墓

谢重辉

生为朝贵客 死作郡先贤

万里家难返 遂埋官道边

丰碑成祖记 遗事野人传

太息松楸尽 牛羊上墓阡

谢重辉，字千仞，号方山，山东德州人。康熙初年官至中书舍人、刑部郎中。著有《杏村集》七卷。谢重辉借回乡之机，凭吊古墓，作五律《苏禄国王墓》，赞誉苏禄东王为"贵客""先贤"，并为彼时陵墓荒芜冷落而"太息"。

苏禄国王墓诗

赵善庆

梯山航海朝丹阙

赤绶金章拜风楼

生寄百蛮居化外

死归万里葬荒丘

层云渺渺魂南望

细雨潇潇水北流

世事以从陵谷变

椒浆欲奠使人愁

赵善庆，字怡斋，德州人，清朝康熙年间由贡生授国子监助教，官至金华府知府。他曾学诗于清初著名学者王士禛，著有《重知堂诗》。赵善庆曾作七律《苏禄国王墓诗》，缅怀苏禄东王"梯山航海"，不远万里来华访问的壮举，表达了对逝者的沉痛哀思。

# Chapter V
# The Descendants of Paduka Pahala Integrating into Chinese Big Family

Everything was well arranged by the Court after Paduka Pahala was buried. His elder son Dumahamn was conferred as East King of Saltanah Sulu, succeeded to the throne and returned to their country with the mission. His queen Kamulin, his second son An Dulu the third son Wen Hala and dozens of the attendants stayed in China as grave keepers. Later, the descendants of Sulu settled, intermarried and bred in the foreign land, and gradually a special clan in Dezhou An-Wen family emerged.

For the members of An-Wen family, there still exists the genes of Sulu in their blood. Even though they have been separated ten thousand miles away. For 600 years, they have been guarding the tomb devotedly and meanwhile sustaining the traditional friendship between China and the Philippines.

# 情系中华

## ——苏禄东王后裔融入中华大家庭

苏禄东王安葬后，明成祖对其后事进行了妥善处理：特封东王长子都麻含为苏禄国东王，继承王位，率团归国；特许东王妃葛木宁与王次子安都鲁、三子温哈刺及从者十人留华守墓，以安慰逝者，昭示来者。从此，苏禄东王在华守墓的后裔繁衍生息，形成了一个特殊的家族——德州安温家族。

相隔几百年，相望几千里。世居中国山东德州的安温家族，身体里依然流淌着苏禄王族的基因，他们悉心守护着苏禄东王墓，同时也在坚守着中菲和平友好关系的传统。

# Paduka Pahala's Queen Consort and Princes Settle in Dezhou as Special Immigrants

## 大明国宾——王妃、王子留居中国德州

After the building of the tomb, Paduka Pahala's wife Kamulin and his second son An Dulu and the third son Wen Hala put forward a request that they would stay to keep the grave for three years, which was ratified by Emperor Zhu Di because it conformed to the Chinese custom.

大明神宗顯皇帝實錄

萬歷三十八年七月辛亥○先是，永樂十五年，蘇祿國王巴都噶叭嗒剌率眷屬與陪臣國人來朝，賜宴賞并印章，封以王爵，伴送回國。秋至德州，王卒。訃聞，遣官營葬于州城北，賜諡恭定，命春秋祭。長子都麻含還本國襲爵，留偏妃葛木寧、次子安都祿等及陪臣國人守其墓，行戶部于德州常豐倉內，照拏生男婦每名口月給廩糧一石、布、鈔等項。即撥歷城德州三姓回回供其役，準免雜差，仍御制碑文勒石。

苏禄东王墓建成后，为了陪伴永眠中华的亲人，东王妃葛木宁与王次子安都鲁、三子温哈剌主动请求留华，为苏禄东王守墓三年。这个请求，与中国儒家文化提倡的孝道相吻合，且符合当时中国的丧葬礼制，因而得到明成祖的特许。

明政府对留华守墓的苏禄东王妃、王子的生活进行了妥善安排，以"国宾"的礼遇给予充分照顾：一是恩赐祭田，保障对苏禄东王的祭祀之需，"恩赐十二城之（地），共祭田二顷三十八亩，永不起科"；二是对守墓人员及其子女按人口数量，每人每月发给粮食一石，以及一定数量的钱、布等，以保障苏禄东王守墓后裔的粮食及生活用品之需；三是特意从历城（今济南）迁来三户回民——马丑斯、陈咬柱、夏乃马，"发给札符，着三户永远相兼看守王墓，供给王裔役使，耕种祭田，供王祀事，全户豁免杂泛差徭"（《温安家乘要录·恤典》）。

按照大明礼制，守孝三年期满后，王妃、王子等守墓人员都可以离华归国。但系于多种情结，三年守制结束后，王妃、王子并未回国，而是继续留居德州。明政府尊重王妃、王子们的选择，礼遇照旧。

永乐二十一年（1423 年），守墓六载的王妃葛木宁提出回国要求，明成祖尊重王妃的选择，"厚赐而遣之"。时隔一年，即永乐二十二年，葛木宁又回到德州，从此便与

Queen Consort and Princes Building Houses and Living beside Tomb, Neighboring the Native Residents with Surname Xia, Ma and Chen

王妃王子与夏、马、陈三户傍墓而居

两位王子继续留居中国。王妃、王子病逝后，安葬于苏禄东王墓东南侧，永远相伴。

王妃、王子们之所以愿意留在中国，应该是由多方面因素促成的。在三年的守墓生活中，他们与当地人和睦相处，适应了在中国的生活，对德州产生了眷恋之情。而且明朝国土辽阔，国家富强文明，经济繁荣发达，人民生活富足；中华文化博大精深，儒家文化讲究仁慈包容、崇礼重义、和谐谦让，这与伊斯兰文化又有相通之处。发达的经济、文化深深吸引了王妃和王子们。他们慕风向化，喜欢、接受并融入其中，遂决心定居德州。

The Ming government arranged the settlement of the descendants of Sultan Paduka Pahala in Dezhou. They were treated as state guests. They were given more than 13 hectares of land, regular pension was supplied to guarantee their daily life, and three Muslim families (Chen Yaozhu, Ma Chousi and Xia Naima and their family) moved to Dezhou from Licheng county to serve them.

According to the Chinese custom, the grave keepers could return home after three years. However, they chose to stay in Dezhou because of some considerations. the Ming government gave them all they needed in China.

Tomb of Queen Consort, Kamulin, Tomb of Prince, An Dulu, Tomb of Prince, Wen Hala

王妃葛木宁与王子安都鲁、温哈刺之墓

**The Bridge of Sino-Philippines Friendship**
Marking the 600th Anniversary of the Visit to China by the Sultans of Sulu

奎章
纪念苏禄王访华六百周年

# The Descendants of Paduka Pahala forming An-Wen Family

## 繁衍生息——苏禄东王后裔形成安温家族

Queen consort Kamulin and princes An Dulu, Wen Hala settled down in Dezhou. Two princes married and bred in their second hometown. Gradually, a new village Beiying came into being.

Marriage acts as a catalytic agent in the process of the ethnic integration. The offspring of Paduka Pahala understood it. Their marriage to the natives

**Today's Tomb of Puduka Pahala and Beiying Village**
今苏禄东王墓及北营村

王妃葛木宁与王子安都鲁、温哈剌在德州定居下来。两位王子娶妻生子，繁衍生息，以耕读为业，代代相袭，把德州当作故乡，安居齐鲁大地，浸润华夏文明，逐步形成了一个守陵村落——北营村。

二王子安都鲁、三王子温哈剌的妻子分别是息剌安、嗒剌一林，这两人显然是苏禄女子，可能是王妃侍女。但从二王子的儿子安里池、三王子的儿子温嗒勿始，即与当地人通婚。安里池娶马氏，温嗒勿娶李氏。此后，其所生各子均与当地女子成亲：安里池长子安世隆，娶妻常氏；次子安世奉，娶妻白氏。温嗒勿长子温玉，娶妻马氏；次子温山，娶妻高氏；三子温鉴，娶妻张氏。

婚姻是民族融合的催化剂，随着婚姻范围的扩大，苏

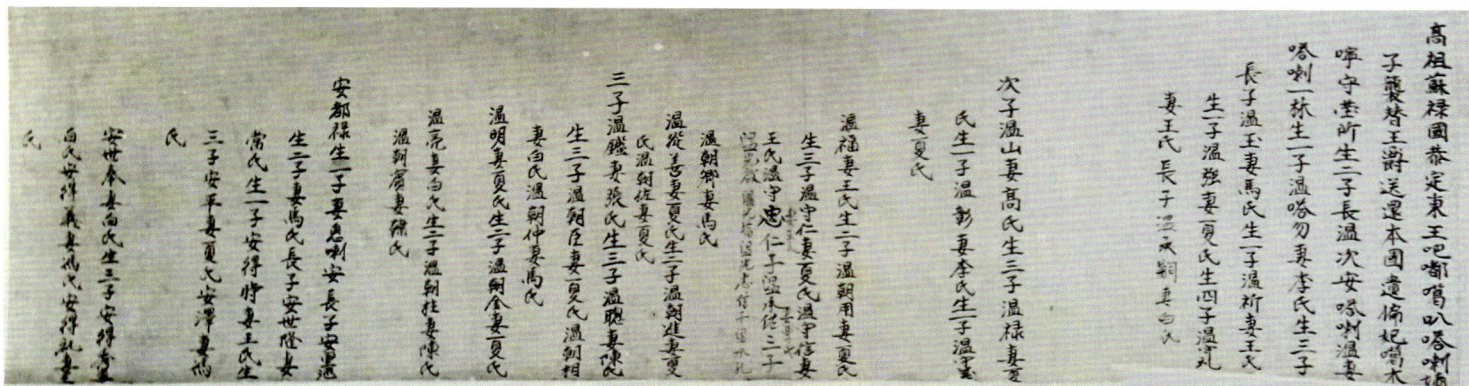

**An-Wen Family Tree** （Shandong Province Museum）
**温安家谱世系**（原件存于山东省博物馆）

从第二代守墓人开始，苏禄东王后裔无论是姓氏还是姓名都逐步中国化。以"安""温"二字为姓，既符合两位王子姓氏译音的第一音节，又符合中国百家姓。他们后代的名字，也都遵照中国取"吉名"的习俗，如温玉、温山，安世隆、安世奉，等等

禄东王后裔与当地人民融合的脚步大大加快。他们吸取了当地家族观念，以父系血缘为纽带，分别取"安""温"为姓，繁衍生息，聚族而居，逐渐形成安、温两脉。

安、温两脉都是苏禄东王巴都葛叭答剌的直系后代，整体上是一个大家族；两脉各自发展，自成世系，因而各自又成为一个家族。经过一百多年的繁衍生息，到明朝万历年间（1573—1620年），安、温二姓已有七十余口人，成为一个比较大的家族。

安温家族继承了先祖苏禄东王的宗教信仰——伊斯兰教。明政府为表示尊重，大约在万历年间，在东王墓西南建立清真寺一座，并明谕"于温安二姓中选举掌教一人，承袭宗派，管理回众"。明崇祯元年（1628年），礼部给东王后裔温守孝颁发札符冠带，并由此形成掌教制。此后，安温家族实行族长制与掌教制双重管理体制。族长一般由安温二姓中德高望重者担任，是家族中的"行政首脑"，负责家族日常杂务：管理族产，制定族规、家法，处理家族内部纠纷，并代表家族与官府及外界交往等。掌教一般由安温二姓中具有高深伊斯兰教经学修养的人担任，是家族中的"精神领袖"，负责宗教事务，包括经堂教育、会礼、诵经祭墓、主持婚礼与葬礼等。

sped up the pace of their integrating into the local community. At the same time, they came to absorb the Chinese concept of family and gradually two patriarchal families with the surname An and Wen respectively emerged.

The members of An-Wen family inherited their ancestor's religious belief. During Wanli period of the Ming Dynasty, the government built a mosque in the southwest side of the tomb. According to the emperor's order, an imam was chosen from the family to govern it. Hence, both clans the An-Wen family was managed by an elder and imam.

**The Bridge of Sino-Philippines Friendship**
Marking the 600th Anniversary of the Visit to China by the Sultans of Sulu

纪念苏禄王访华六百周年

# The Descendants of Paduka Pahala Officially Became Naturalized Citizens of the Qing Dynasty

## 入籍德州——苏禄东王后裔正式成为大清编户

From the Yongle's period of the Ming Dynasty to the early Qing Period, the Sulu descendants kept interacting with the natives, integrating themselves into the local society and learning from them. Over more than 300 years, they became localized.

大清世宗憲皇帝實錄

雍正十一年癸丑六月戊午○禮部議復：蘇祿國王臣母漢末母拉律林奏稱：伊祖東王，於明永樂年間來朝，歸至山東德州病故。所有墳墓及其子孫存留賜邮之處。經今三百餘年，廢墜已久，懇請修理給復。臣部行文山東巡撫飭查。……查蘇祿國遠隔重洋，感戴皇上德化，進表謝恩，爲伊遠祖墳墓，子孫懇請整理給復，情詞懇切，應如所請。令山東巡撫轉飭德州地方官，清查蘇祿國王墓址，所有神道、享亭、牌坊等項，修葺整理。於安溫二族之中，遴取稍通文墨者各一人爲奉祀生，給與頂戴，永以爲例。並知照該國王可也。從之。

苏禄王后裔最初是以客居的形式留居中国，享受明政府恩赐的田产、俸禄和王族特权。从明朝永乐年间到清朝初年，经过三百余年的繁衍生息，安温家族与当地人民接触、融合，学习当地人民的耕织技术和经商经验，从事各种营生，逐渐"华化"。到清朝初年，他们在语言、民俗、生产方式、生活状况等方面，已经和当地人民相差无几。雍正年间，苏禄王后裔正式"以温、安为姓，入籍德州"，成为清朝的编户齐民，从而结束了在华客居时代，成为中华大家庭的一员。

苏禄王后裔入籍中国，是长期融合的结果，符合苏禄王后裔的诉求，而清初与苏禄政治联系的恢复与加强，则为苏禄王后裔入籍中国奠定了良好的外部条件。

清雍正五年（1727年），苏禄国再次入华朝贡。当时，苏禄国王母汉末母拉律林委派中国商人龚廷彩为苏禄访华使团的正使，由驸马阿石丹任副使，带着"国书"和大批的礼品，到中国进行访问。在访华过程中，苏禄使团遵照苏禄国王母汉末母拉律林的指示，专程到德州拜谒了东王陵墓，会见了东王第八代孙安汝奇、温崇楷等人。历经三百多年的风雨硝烟，东王陵墓和庙宇已荒芜废圮。此时留华守墓的安温家族已繁衍至一百九十二人，但仍以"宾客"身份居于德州。安汝奇、温崇楷为此向龚廷彩、阿石丹提出三方面的诉求：一是修葺东王陵庙；二是希望恢复明万历年间已被停发的每人每月的俸粮；三是结束客居身份，入籍德州。龚廷彩、阿石丹答应回苏禄后如实向国王转达。

雍正十年（1732 年），苏禄国王母汉末母拉律林再次派龚廷彩为使臣访华。使团于雍正十一年（1733 年）六月到达北京，向雍正皇帝呈上苏禄国王的信件，信中对上次使团访华所受到的隆重接待和馈赠，表达了深切的谢意，同时向雍正皇帝提出了修葺东王陵庙、眷恤苏禄东王后裔的请求。雍正皇帝非常重视，命山东地方官员对苏禄东王墓的陵、庙、神道、享亭、牌坊进行整修；令安汝奇、温崇楷为族长，看守坟墓；恢复明代春、秋二祭，并从苏禄东王后裔——安、温二姓中各遴选一名"奉祀生"，赐予顶戴，主持王墓祭奠；允许苏禄东王后裔以温、安为姓，就地落籍，入籍德州。

安、温家族入籍德州，标志着苏禄东王后裔结束了在华客居的时代，正式成为清朝的在籍编户。这是苏禄东王后裔与当地居民逐渐融合的历史结果，在中菲友好交流的历史上点缀上精彩的一笔。

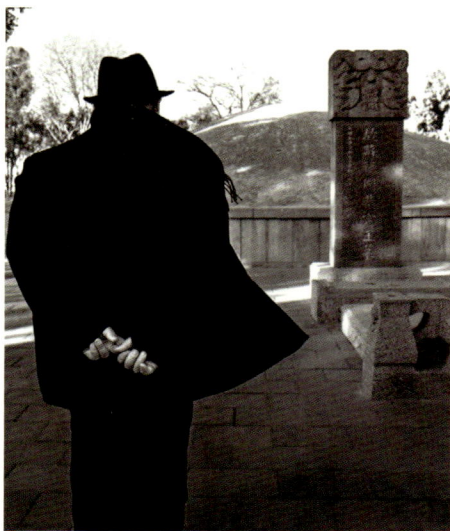

〔乾隆〕德州志卷十一

國朝雍正五年，國王來朝。九年國王蘇老丹折奏禮部，查明前明留德守墓人等子孫，以溫安爲姓入籍德州，題定二姓各立奉祀生一名，該撫題明嫡系承襲，給照在案。十年，發帑金修其墓。

Until the early period of the Qing Dynasty, they had nearly no differences in the language, the custom, the mode of production and the living condition etc. During the reign of Emperor Yongzheng, they got the registered permanent residents of Dezhou and became naturalized citizens of China. Their sojourning life as immigrants have ended.

**Tomb Keeper, Mr. An Jinming, the 17th Offspring of Puduka Pahala**

八十三岁高龄的安金明老先生是苏禄东王后裔第十七代孙，守墓人的角色伴随了他的一生。当他迈着迟暮而康健的步伐走向苏禄王墓时，仿佛是嵌入了六百年前的时空

**The Bridge of Sino-Philippines Friendship**
Marking the 600th Anniversary of the Visit to China by the Sultans of Sulu

奎章

纪念苏禄王访华十六百周年

# The Cultural Heritage and Ethics Standards of The An-Wen Family

## 崇儒尚义——安温家族的家学与门风

An-Wen family not only inherited the Muslim culture of the Philippines, but accepted the Chinese traditional Confucianism, which set an example for Sino-Philippine cultural relationship and integration.

At the age of the late Ming and early Qing Dynasty, the modes of production and life of the An-Wen family changed overall under the influence of Confucianism. They focused on the importance of agriculture and reading. Their youths were all struggling for the imperial examination and the family was proud of them.

From the Ming and Qing Dynasty to the Republic of China, the literary writers and the officials emerged constantly out of An-Wen family such as An Shousun, Wen Pan, An Ruqi, Wen Chongkai, Wen Li, An

安温家族既继承了菲律宾传统的伊斯兰文化，又逐渐接受中国传统的儒家文化，从而形成了以伊斯兰教为基本信仰、以传统儒学家法为门风、具有南洋穆斯林血统的独特家族，成为中菲文化交流融合的典范。

明末清初，安温家族的生产、生活方式发生了全面转型，逐步接受了儒家文化，以耕读传家。尤其是清初入籍中国以后，安温家族正式成为中华大家庭的一员，崇儒之风日盛。安、温子弟纷纷进入府、州、县学，参加科考，以儒学光耀门庭。

从明、清到民国，安温家族秀才、举人相继，名卿辈出，

**Wen Xian, the Learned Offspring of Sulu East King**
**温宪像**

清乾隆六十年（1795年），温宪参加山东乡试，"棘闱"胜出，荣登"桂榜"，成为家族第二位举人。初任河南修武县知县，为民兴利除害、廉洁勤政。因"才知干练"，不断升迁，先后在安徽的池州、宁国、安庆等地任官，后升凤阳知府、庐凤道台

如安守孙、温泮、安汝奇、温崇楷、温立、安永久、温德荣、安泰、温宪、温如盘、安福海等。他们通"四书"、贯"五经"，以"修身、齐家、治国、平天下"为理想，以经邦治国为己任，长于诗赋，学养深厚，或出仕为官，或聚徒授学，为家族及当地人民所推崇，为儒学的传播与传承做出了贡献。士大夫风尚遂在家族内部逐步形成。

安温家族不仅有崇礼尚义的儒风，还有慷慨任侠的传统。他们崇尚"忠义""气节"与"风骨"，形成家族慷慨侠义之风。如"马革裹尸"的清代将领安玉魁，民国时期爱国将领安树德、安树仁、安舜，正义商人温寿文，血洒疆场的抗日英烈安德馨等人，至今仍令人称道。

门风永续，生生不息。从明永乐年间至今六百年，苏禄东王在华后裔已繁衍至第二十一代，在世者有三千七百余人，分布上呈现出大分散、小集中的格局。安温家族的主体集中于德州北营村，其他成员则广泛分布于山东德州、兖州、淄博，河北保定、东光、吴桥、沧州，河南开封、焦作，安徽蚌埠，以及天津、北京、哈尔滨、贵阳、昆明、兰州、

Yongjiu, Wen Derong, An Tai, Wen Xian, Wen Rupan, An Fuhai, etc. They were proficient in The Four Books and The Five Classics and internalized the Confucian ideal that urged individuals to "cultivate the moral self, regulate the family, run the state rightly and make the world peaceful". Some chose to be officials, some chose to open the home school, and no matter what they were engaged in, they were all popular with their family and the local residents.

The family members absorbed the essence from Qi-Lu and Yan-Zhao cultures, and advocated moral courage and patriotic loyalty, of whom some were thought highly of by the later generations such as An Yukui, a general in the Qing Dynasty who died on the battlefield, An Shude, An Shuren and An Shun, the patriotic generals in the period of the Republic of China, Wen Shouwen, a righteous businessman and An Dexin, a hero in anti-Japanese war, and so on and so forth.

← An Shude, a Patriotic General and Enterpreneur
安树德像（1927年拍摄）

安树德（1894—1950），字润身，苏禄东王第十五代孙，民国时期著名回族将领和爱国商人。青年时期，跟随冯玉祥南征北战，官至国民革命军第二集团军第十八师中将师长，镇守西北边陲。冯玉祥下野后，安树德先后创办了一大批民族企业

→ An Shude's Tomb
安树德墓

## Wen Shouwen, a Patriotic Enterpreneur
### 温寿文像

温寿文（1871—1947），字焕章，苏禄东王第十六代孙。
20世纪20年代在徐州开设保新面粉厂，自任经理。因经营有术，工厂日益发展壮大，多设分厂、经销处。1937年抗日战争全面爆发后，后温寿文主动关闭工厂，毅然回乡。于1934年编成《温安家乘要录》

During the 600 years from the Yongle period of the Ming Dynasty up to now, the descendants of Paduka Pahala in China have multiplied to the 21<sup>st</sup> generation with the population of more than 3,700. The members are dispersed across the country, but most are living in Dezhou. On the annual Memorial Day of the East King of Sulu, representatives of his descendants from across the country gathered in Dezhou, and held a grand sacrificial ceremony.

In 2014, some descendants from Beiying village, Dezhou, organized a committee to compile their family tree and it took nearly three years to make it. This work entitled *Family Tree of Paduka Pahala's Descendants in China* is mainly based on An-Wen family in Dezhou. There are 25 branches across the country all-included. It is the most integral pedigree in their family history, reflection of their genuine life and inheritance of their parental instructions of loyalty, obedience, tenderness

太原、西宁、沈阳、营口、台北等地。每年苏禄东王祭日，全国苏禄东王后裔代表齐聚德州，睦族联宗，举行家祭大典。

为传承家学，睦族联宗，2014年，德州北营苏禄东王后裔发起成立全国苏禄东王后裔温安通谱编委会。经过近三年时间，温安通谱编纂完成并定名为《中华·苏禄东王家族通谱》。通谱以德州北营温安"根脉"为主体，囊括全国二十五大支脉三十一个地区，是有史以来最全的一部温安家谱。通谱是继明末《温安家谱》、民国《温安家乘要录》、2006年《安氏族谱》之后的第四部温安家谱，是苏禄东王在华后裔六百年繁衍生息的写照，传承着"敬主、忠顺、温厚、善良"的祖训，并赋予其新的内涵："对国家忠心耿耿，报效奉献；对亲朋温和善良，诚实守信；对教门虔诚奉行，乐善好施；对世人谦虚礼让，宽容大度；对族人尊敬帮扶，亲善和睦。"彰显时代内涵，爱国爱教，传承家训，弘扬民族团结。

Offspring Representatives across the Country Gathering in Front of the Tomb
来自全国各地的苏禄东王后裔代表齐聚苏禄东王墓祭祖

and kindness. And nowadays their parental instructions are endowed with the new connotation: loyal to the nation, kind to family and friends, honest and faithful, devoted to belief, happy in doing good, generous, respectful to the clansmen.

The An-Wen family benefited a lot from their parental heritageand as a result, men of talent come out in succession such as An Diwei, a famous scholar, Vice Chairman of the Chinese People's Political Consultative Conference of Guizhou Province; An Diguang, a distinguished medical scientist, professor of Academy of Traditional Chinese Medicine of China; An Wenxuan, a senior engineer, Vice Chairman of the Chinese People's Political Consultative Conference of Kaifeng City; Wen Xihai, a senior engineer, model worker; Wen Yongming, a well-known entrepreneur, and An Junfeng, an eminent educationist and so on, all of whom are pride of the their family.

温安家学得以发扬，家族人才辈出，如著名学者、贵州省政协副主席安迪伟，著名医学家、中国中医研究院教授安迪光，高级工程师、开封市政协副主席安文选，高级工程师、劳动模范温锡海，知名企业家温永明，著名教育家安俊峰等，他们都是东王后裔的骄傲。

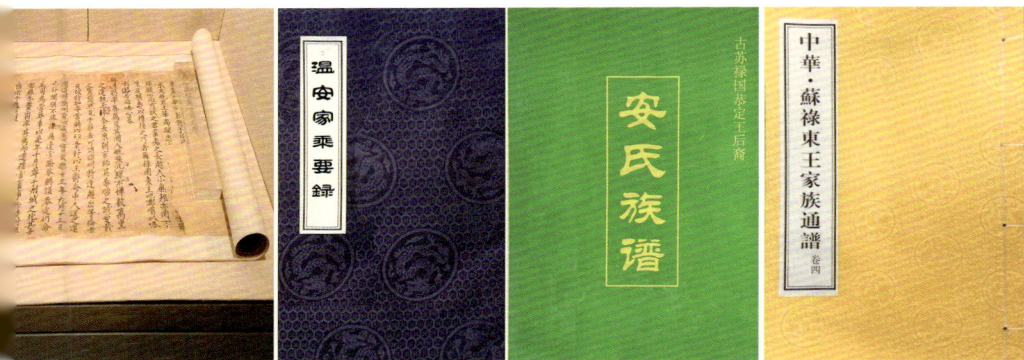

Offsprings' Family Tree
苏禄东王后裔历代家谱

# Chapter VI
## Chinese and Filipinos Cherishing the Past and Promoting Further Friendship

The Sulu Sultans' visit to China started a new era for the political, economic and cultural exchanges between China and the Philippines. From then on, other states in the Philippine islands in Luzon like Pangasinan followed.

This historical event 600 years ago witnessed the friendly ties between China and the foreign, showing the peaceful diplomatic notion of the old Chinese empire. Today the proposal of the Belt and Road by the Chinese government accords with the spirits reflected by the old Maritime Silk Road. History has been integrated perfectly with today; tradition and inheritance have been sublimated.

# 继往开来

## ——中菲人民珍视历史增进友谊

苏禄王访华，开启了中菲政治、经济及文化交流的新时期。在此前后，菲律宾群岛诸国，如吕宋、冯嘉施兰、合猫里、猫里务、网巾礁老、古麻剌朗、沙瑶、呐哔啴等，也纷纷入华访问。

几百年前的不辞万里艰辛，展现出的是一曲曲中外友好交流的"盛世华章"，于古代，它呼应的是中国国力强盛和友好盛情的外交理念；于今天，它更是古代海上丝绸之路与"一带一路"倡议的有机契合，是跨越时空的心灵相通。友好交往的历史在今天得到传承与升华。

**The Bridge of Sino-Philippines Friendship**
Marking the 600th Anniversary of the Visit to China by the Sultans of Sulu

奎章
纪念苏禄王访华六百周年

# The Continuation and Development of Sino-Philippines Friendship

## 友谊永续——中菲友好交往延续和发展

The funeral affairs were well arranged at the Emperor's directive after Paduka Pahala's death. At the same time, the domestic regime of Sulu was arranged as well, for instance, Paduka Pahala's eldest son, Du Mahan was sent back to succeed to the throne and guarantee the political stability in the Philippine Islands.

苏禄东王去世后，明成祖对东王后事进行了妥善处理。在安置东王守墓人员的同时，明成祖对苏禄国内政权的交接也做了妥善安排，敕命随团访华的东王长子都麻含继承王位，回国即位，以保障苏禄的政治安定。为此，明成祖谆谆教诲都麻含，继承父志，敬承天道，以德治国，以礼服人。

明成祖对苏禄东王后事、留华守墓人员的生活及苏禄政权交接的妥善处理，深得苏禄国君臣和人民的赞赏与感激，为明政府与苏禄关系的继续发展奠定了基础。之后，双方关系继续朝着良好的方向发展。

大明太宗文皇帝實錄

永樂十五年九月乙丑○遣使賚敕，諭其長子都麻含曰：『爾父知尊中國，躬率家屬、陪臣，經涉海道，萬里來朝。眷其誠悃，已賜王封，優加賜賚，遣人護送還國。舟次德州，以疾殁。朕聞之，良用憫悼，已葬祭如禮。爾以嫡長，為國人所屬，宜即繼承，以綏藩服。今特命爾為蘇祿國東王，爾尚益懋忠貞，敬承天道，以副眷懷，以承爾父之志。欽哉！』

永乐十八年（1420年）八月，苏禄国西王麻哈剌叱葛剌麻丁遣使来华访问。明政府按照惯例，礼尚往来，厚赐西王使节，以鼓励苏禄使节来华，巩固和加强双方的友好往来。

永乐十九年（1421年）四月，苏禄东王母遣王叔叭都加苏哩来华访问，朝见明成祖，对明成祖给予苏禄东王生前、死后的礼遇表示感激。东王母，即前东王巴都葛叭答剌的正妻。对于东王母遣王叔来华访问，明成祖给予了很高的礼遇，除赐给文锦、纱罗、彩绢等物品外，还赐予了与一般使节不同的"冠带""袭衣"等，以示尊崇。

永乐二十一年（1423年），守墓六载的东王妃葛木宁回国，明成祖"厚赐而遣之"。但葛木宁出于对德州——苏禄东王长眠之地的眷恋，时隔一年又回到中国，与两位王子继续留居德州。对此，明政府表示欢迎，并对王妃进行了妥善安置。

The Sulu government was contented and thought highly of what the Ming Dynasty did in this matter, which is to lay the foundation for the development of the bilateral ties.

After Emperor Zhu Di died, Ming's amicable diplomatic policy continued. Good ties with Sulu continued which objectively supplied the relatives of Paduka Pahala in China with the good external conditions.

In the Qing Dynasty, the government inherited the diplomatic policy of good neighborly and friendly relations.

大明太宗文皇帝實錄
永樂十八年秋八月乙卯
○蘇祿國西王麻哈剌叱葛剌麻丁遣陪臣奉表，貢方物。賜鈔幣遣還。

大明太宗文皇帝實錄
永樂十九年夏四月癸卯○蘇祿國東王之母遣王叔叭都加蘇哩等貢方物。賜叭都加蘇哩冠帶、襲衣、鈔、紵絲、文錦、紗羅、彩絹，賜其從人有差。

大明宣宗章皇帝實錄

洪熙元年冬十二月己丑〇賜奉使蘇禄等國回還官軍千户汪海等九十五人鈔幣、表裏布有差。宣德二年冬十月壬戌〇賜奉使蘇禄等國回還福州左等衛千户趙清等及朝鮮國使臣安壽山、金乙賢等四十一人鈔、彩、幣、表裏綿布有差。

大明仁宗昭皇帝實錄

永樂二十二年冬十月丁巳〇蘇禄等國遣頭目生亞烈巴欲等貢方物。賜襲衣、鈔幣有差。

*Scene of Tens of Thousands of Vassal States Having an Audience with Chinese Emperor, Qianlong Period, Qing Dynasty* (Part)

乾隆《万国来朝图》（局部）

明成祖去世以后，明政府延续传统的"厚往薄来"政策，发展同菲律宾群岛诸国的友好关系，苏禄与中国继续保持着政治、经济的友好往来。明仁宗时，苏禄等国来华访问，答谢明政府对苏禄东王及其留华后裔的礼遇。仁宗厚赐苏禄使节。

明宣宗时，中国两次派使节出使苏禄等国，加强与菲律宾群岛诸国的联系。洪熙元年（1425年）十二月，明宣宗派遣千户汪海等出使苏禄等国；宣德二年（1427年），又遣千户赵清等人出使苏禄等国。

明代，中国与苏禄始终保持着密切的政治联系与经济、文化交流，成为当时中国对外关系的典范。两国友好关系的延续，也为客居德州的苏禄东王守墓人员提供了良好的外部环境。

清政府秉承明朝"怀夷柔远"的外交传统，实行以友好往来为宗旨的外交政策。康、雍、乾三朝屡次遣使晓谕南洋诸国，得到周边诸国的响应，外国使节纷至杳来。清代诗人陶元藻在他的《题十三国番夷图》诗中曾用"鳞鳞筶屋绕溪间，汶莱苏禄争低昂"的诗句来描述当时各国来华的盛况。

雍正四年（1726年），苏禄遣使来华，恢复了因战乱而一度中断的政治联系。雍正、乾隆二朝，双方政治、经济、文化交流颇为频繁。

16世纪后期，苏禄国面临着西班牙的殖民侵略。自1578年开始，西班牙殖民者多次进攻苏禄的和乐岛，威胁苏禄的对外贸易。1721年、1722年和1723年，西班牙殖民者先后三次进攻和乐岛，苏禄面临着被占领的危险。正是在苏禄抗击西班牙殖民侵略的危急时刻，苏禄国王母汉末母拉律林于1727年委派旅居苏禄的华商龚廷彩为正使，驸马阿石丹为副使，入华访问。

龚廷彩原是中国福建泉州人，康熙年间到吕宋经商，由于资金耗尽，不得不逗留海外，后来去了苏禄。龚廷彩向苏禄国王母汉末母拉律林详细介绍了清朝富庶强盛的情况，而当时苏禄人民正进行着长期不懈的反抗西班牙侵略的斗争，很想恢复同中国的联系并得到中国的帮助。母汉末母拉律林听了龚廷彩的介绍后，委任他为正使，苏禄人阿石丹为副使，与通事（翻译）杨佩宁及大小属吏共十一人组成访华使团，带着表文（国书）、礼品到中国进行访问。龚廷彩一行于雍正四年（1726年）七月到达泉州港。十月，雍正皇帝接到闽浙总督高其倬关于苏禄使团到达福建的报告，非常重视，下令高其倬派专人护送至京，并通知沿途地方官员妥善照料。龚廷彩一行于雍正五年（1727年）六月到达北京，向雍正皇帝进呈表文。表文深切表达了苏禄国王希望两国通好的诚挚愿望。

苏禄国王的奏表诚恳之至，雍正帝非常高兴，随即致函苏禄国王，一方面对苏禄国王遣使访华表示钦佩和赞赏，另一方面也表达了对进一步发展双方友好往来的期冀，希望传承历史，友谊永续。

**欽定大清會典**

凡四夷朝貢之國，東曰朝鮮，東南曰琉球、蘇祿，南曰安南、暹羅，西南曰西洋、緬甸、南掌。

**大清世宗憲皇帝實錄**

雍正五年丁未六月丙申○蘇祿國王蘇老丹臣母漢末母拉律林表言：臣僻居荒服，遠隔神京，幸際昌期，末由趨覲。邇來天無烈風霆雨，海不揚波，知中國必有聖人。臣捧閱歷朝紀事，原有觀光之例。是用遣使臣龔廷彩、阿石丹，奉臣赤心，仰陳彤陛，敬獻本國所產土物，聊效野人負暄之意。

In the 4th year of Emperor Yongzheng, Sulu dispatched the envoys to China to renew the bilateral political ties. During the period of Yongzheng and Qianlong reigns, the envoys were sent to China many times, and the political and economic exchanges were most active.

Sulu Sultans' visit to China as a bridge of friendship has been a symbol

**大清世宗憲皇帝實錄**

雍正五年丁未六月丙申○敕諭蘇禄國王母漢末母拉律林：朕惟職貢虔修，爲臣輸忠之大義，寵施弘錫，大國柔遠之常經，越母漢末母拉律林，屬在退陬，克舒丹悃，敬恭遣使，梯航不隔于重海以瞻云，識向風之有素，宜加賚予，以勵蓋誠。是用重海以瞻云，識向風之有素，宜加賚予，以勵蓋誠。是用降敕獎諭，懇切陳詞，琛贄並將其方物，慕義之忱，良可嘉尚。滄溟，懇切陳詞，並賜王文綺、器皿等物。王其祇受，益矢恪恭，副朕降敕獎諭，並賜王文綺、器皿等物。王其祇受，益矢恪恭，副朕眷懷。至王所請貢期，念爾國遠在重洋，往來迢遞，酌俟五年之外，一修歲獻之儀，若王有所敷陳，則隨時上達。故茲敕諭。

雍正皇帝命礼部举行盛大的宴会招待苏禄使团。同年七月，在午门举行隆重仪式，赠予苏禄国王蟒缎六匹、青蓝彩缎十匹、蓝素缎十匹、锦六匹、绸十匹、衣素缎十匹、闪缎八匹、罗十匹、纱十匹。厚赏正、副使龚廷彩、阿石丹，通事杨佩宁等。苏禄使团在福建登船返国前，清政府又在福州举行了盛大的送行宴会。

雍正十年（1732年），苏禄国王母汉末母拉律林再次派遣龚廷彩入华朝贡，上表感谢清政府对前次苏禄使团的接待和赏赐。清政府依照惯例厚赐来使，双方关系继续发展。

乾隆时期，双方通使更加频繁，关系更为密切。乾隆五年（1740年），苏禄国王麻喊末呵禀勝咛派专人护送在海上遇风暴的难民蔡长茂、杨兴发等二十五人回福建，并请求"入贡"。乾隆皇帝接报后当即表示欢迎，对苏禄的诚意表示嘉许，同意苏禄国国王派遣使团访华。为此，乾隆皇帝特意下令，命沿途地方官对将要来华访问的苏禄使团加意照看，以示诚意。

乾隆七年（1742年），苏禄国王麻喊末呵禀勝咛派遣正使马光明、副使勝独喊敏、通事陈朝盛出访中国，九月二十一日到达厦门。乾隆八年（1743年），苏禄使者到达北京。在京期间，受到清政府的友好接待。乾隆皇帝特别叮嘱礼部官员："今年天气炎热，苏禄国使臣等在京，著礼部派官员加意照看，多给冰水及解暑药物，并遣医人不时看视。"（《清高宗实录》卷一九三）六月，乾隆皇帝在正大光明殿接见了苏禄使团，并给予丰厚的赏赐。

此后，乾隆十二年（1747年）、乾隆十七年（1752年）苏禄国使臣相继使华，双方关系更加密切。乾隆十八年（1753年）十月，苏禄国王嘛喊味麻安柔律嶙派遣唠独万喳剌为使，搭乘福建杨大成的商船来华，"贡方物，并贡国土一包，请以户口、人丁编入中国图籍"。乾隆皇帝接到报告后指出："所奏愿以疆土、人民、户口编入图籍之处，该国远隔重洋，原可无庸准其内附，但若因此又行驳回，令其远涉波涛，非国家柔远之道。此时且不必拒绝，第照例料理来京。俟唠独万喳剌到后，交与部臣定议，再降谕旨。"

苏禄使者到达北京，呈上苏禄国王嘛喊味麻安柔律嶙的《苏禄国王乞隶版图表》，乞请归附中华，言辞恳切。乾隆皇帝考虑到虽然两国世代交好，但海洋阻隔，相距太远；且苏禄内争，西方殖民者插足，形势复杂，须慎重处理。经部议，乾隆帝做出答复："览王奏，进贡方物，具见悃忱。尔国远隔重洋，输诚向化，良可嘉尚。所请将疆土、人丁、

大清高宗純皇帝實錄

乾隆五年庚申九月壬辰〇得旨：蘇禄國隔越重洋，道路遙遠，該國王傾心向化，奏請朝貢，并將失風商船送回內地，其屬可嘉，著准其所請。俟使臣來時，地方官加意照看，以副朕柔遠之意。

Qianlong, Chinese Emperor of the Qing Dynasty, Enjoined the Officials of Ministry Of Rites to take good care of the Sulu Mission in 1743

乾隆上谕（出自《上谕档》）

乾隆八年五月二十六日内阁奉
上谕慶復著補授川陝總督馬爾泰著補授兩廣總督張允隨著授為雲南總督迎撫管事務欽此

乾隆八年五月二十六日内阁奉
上谕直隷宣化鎮總兵官李質粹著補授廣西提督譚行義著調補宣化鎮總兵官欽此

乾隆八年五月二十六日内阁奉
上谕今年天氣炎熱蘇禄國使臣等在京著禮部沁官員加意照著多給氷水及解暑藥物並遣醫人不時看視欽此

乾隆八年五月二十八日内阁奉
上谕前屢用中到部引見朕已降旨交與尹總著以知縣用矣令閩該員在粤西年久熟悉苗疆風土著仍發往廣西

of good relationship of China and the Philippines. Since 1949, especially since the Philippines built the diplomatic relations with the People's Republic of China, the leaders of two countries have paid much attention to this period of long standing history, and both hope to inherit the past and forge a good future.

## Document: Sulu Sultan Asked to Join the Chinese Empire

### 苏禄国王乞隶版图表

苏禄国臣苏老丹嘛喊味麻安柔律嶙为谨陈披赤输诚仰祈睿鉴事。念臣先祖父致竭厥诚于雍正四年、乾隆五年，幸邀天宠，敕许入贡，颁赐龙珍，荣及子孙。迨臣嗣位，旦夕惕厉，思继先志，以永国祚，而贻后世。……惟是焚香北拜，敬遣亲臣万查剌，赍奉表章国土物件，伏望鉴臣赤心。……仰冀皇帝陛下大德敦化，中外咸怀保赤，鸿恩远播，夷狄尽欲子来。臣愿以疆土、人丁、户口编入中国图籍，听任指挥……倘蒙钧旨喜纳，恭候纶音天降，臣来年编籍晋上，即为中国黎元。伏恳矜臣部落荒陬，实表远人之慕化，委质事君，窃比葵藿之倾心。乞施怀柔至意，不胜受恩感激。

乾隆十八年七月
苏禄国臣苏老丹嘛喊味麻安柔律嶙跪奏

户口编入中国之处，已允部议，毋庸赍送图籍。"乾隆皇帝对苏禄国王的"输诚向化"表示赞赏有加，对苏禄王提出的以户口、人丁编入中国版籍一事，则婉言谢绝。

乾隆皇帝致苏禄苏丹嘛喊味麻安柔律嶙的敕谕，表明清政府延续了历代"绥抚四海、厚往薄来"的和平外交政策，但清政府绝无染指领土、干涉内政之意。对于这一点，苏禄国王心悦诚服。此后，两国关系继续发展，成为清代中国与南洋诸国关系的典范。清朝政府对苏禄的支持和援助，鼓舞了苏禄国民众奋起抗击西方殖民者的入侵。在当时，菲律宾群岛上的其他国家纷纷被西班牙殖民者占领，但苏禄仍在较长时间里保持了独立地位。

## Letter from Emperor Qianlong to Sulu Sultan

乾隆皇帝致苏禄苏丹嘛喊味麻安柔律嶙敕谕（出自《上谕档》）

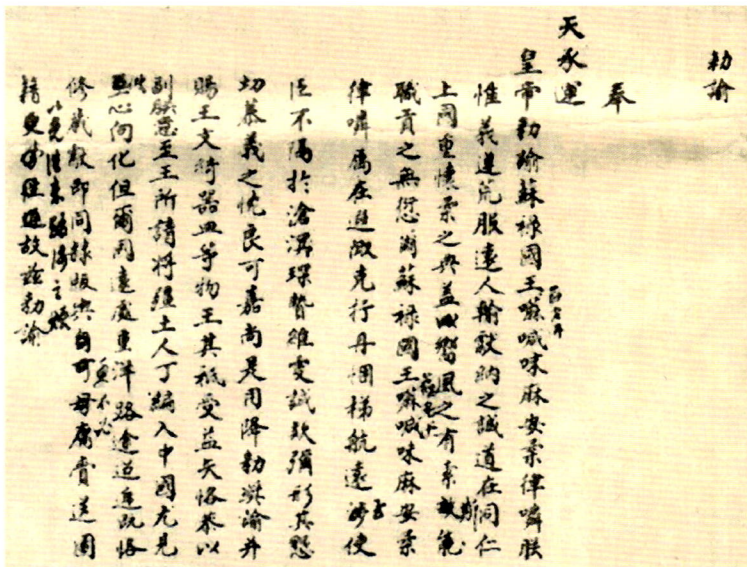

# Continuing Relationship and Mutual Visits between Sino-Philippines Descendants of Sulu Sultan

## 寻根祭祖——中菲苏禄王后裔交流互访

自明代以来，留居中国的苏禄东王后裔——德州安温家族与远在菲律宾的苏禄东王后裔，各自繁衍，时有联系。1949 年新中国成立以来，尤其是 1975 年中菲建交后，随着两国政治、经济、文化交往日益密切，苏禄东王远隔重洋的两支后裔终于相逢在一起，实现了长达近六个世纪跨国血脉的相认相连，构架起中菲人民友谊的桥梁。

1995 年 12 月，菲律宾苏禄东王后裔依氏麦·基兰先生应苏禄东王在中国后裔第十七代孙安金明、安金智、温如安的邀请来德州访问。12 月 3 日，安金明等人早早站在村口迎接，依氏麦·基兰迎着安金明的

Since the Ming Dynasty, the descendants of Paduka Pahala in China and his offsprings in the Philippines have been keeping the constant close touch, which set up a friendly bridge between two countries. Especially since the People's Republic of China was founded; the mutual visits have never ceased.

At the end of 1995, Ismail Kiram, descendant of Sulu Sultan, paid a visit to Dezhou at the invitation of An Jinming, An Jinzhi and Wen Ru'an (17th generation grandsons of Paduka Pahala). On the early morning of 3rd of December, An Jinming waited for Mr. Ismail Kiram at the en-

Mr. Ismail Kiram Came to China and was welcomed warmly by the offsprings of Paduka Pahala, Mr. An Jinming and his family.

菲律宾苏禄王后裔依氏麦·基兰先生来到中国，瞻拜祖墓。时年六十一岁的安金明老先生在家接待了这位同胞，被他珍藏的一组照片记录了当时交流的场景

奎章

纪念苏禄王访华六百周年

**Prince Kiram wrote the Grateful Letter to the Chinese Offspring**

基兰王子留言

trance to the village. When they met, two old men hugged firmly together, tears out of eyes. Later a grand feast was held in An Jinming's home, at which Ismail Kiram said they were blood relatives sharing the same ancestor, that Emperor Zhu Di and Paduka Pahala both hoped the friendship would pass on from generation to generation and that it was their responsibility to maintain it forever.

In September 1999, offspring of Sulu Sultan, Mr. Maruhr Kiram came to Dezhou to offer sacrifices to his ancestor. Maruhr Kiram and the members of An and Wen family had a joyous gathering, and both sides hoped sincerely to pass on and strengthen the friendship.

**Mr. Maruhr Kiram Made a Speech on the Memorial Ceremony.**

苏禄苏丹贾马鲁尔·基拉梅在纪念活动上致辞

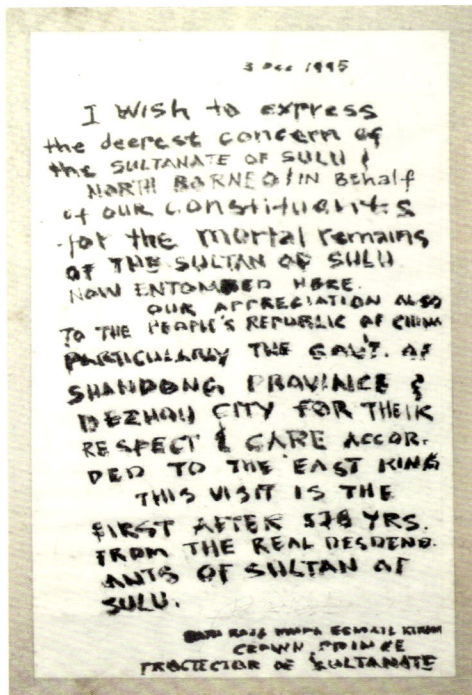

目光缓缓走来。长达近六个世纪跨国血脉的相逢，使两位老人紧紧拥抱，热泪纵横。在安金明家中举行的家宴上，基兰先生说：五百多年下来，我们是同根同宗，明成祖和苏禄王希望中国和苏禄世代友好下去，我们要继续维护和发展中菲友谊，让她世世代代相传下去。

1999 年 9 月，菲律宾苏禄东王后裔贾马鲁尔·基拉梅先生来到中国德州祭祖。他与苏禄东王的德州后裔欢聚一堂，并一起祭扫了苏禄东王墓。中菲两国的苏禄东王后裔共同缅怀苏禄东王，希望加强双方的交流与往来，将中菲友好关系世代传承。

2005 年适逢中菲建交三十周年，中国的苏禄东王后裔

第十七代孙安金田，第十八代孙安砚春、温海军前往菲律宾，踏上寻根之旅。虽然 1949 年以来，在菲律宾的苏禄东王后裔多次应邀到中国德州拜祭先王陵墓、探望异国同根，但中国的苏禄东王后裔探访菲律宾，这在五百八十八年来还是第一次。到达苏禄后，安金田三人参观了苏禄王国最重要的历史遗迹——苏禄王宫遗址。看到先王墓碑，三名来自中国的苏禄东王后裔匍匐在地，长跪不起。五百八十八年后，漂泊在外的苏禄东王后裔终于回到了故土。在先王墓碑附近，安金田、安砚春、温海军立下纪念碑，

On June 10th, 2005, An Jintian (17th generation grandson), and An Yanchun, Wen Haijun (18th generation grandson) went to the Philippines and set off the root seeking tour. The friendly relations between China and the Philippine have never ceased for hundreds of years, but it was the first time for the Chinese descendants to visit the Philippines. There they attended the welcoming ceremony that the Vice Governor of Sulu Province presided over and then visited the most important historic site—Sultan Palace relics. An Jintian, a 76 years old man, knelt down before the ancestor's tomb. A stone tablet was built up by Chinese offsprings besides the tomb, on which the characters were carved to record this significant event. During their stay, President Gloria Macapagal-Arroyo and Romulo, minister of Foreign

The Descendants of Both Countries Worshiped Their Ancestor before the Tomb of Sulu Sultan in Philippines
中菲苏禄王后裔共同祭祖

Three Descendants From China Took Picture Before the Tomb of Sulu Sultan in the Philippines
三位来自中国德州的苏禄王后裔在先王墓前合影留念

Affairs took time from the busy schedules to receive them. Then President Arroyo inquired something about their life and work in China, expressed her gratitude to China government and meanwhile hoped that the friendship between China and the Philippines would last forever.

In July 2007, Mr. Bahjin from Sulu paid a visit to Dezhou. The descendants of the two countries offered the sacrificesto their ancestor in the Islamic traditional way. Bahjin expressed his gratitude to what Chinese government has done for constructing and protecting his ancestor's tombs.

In December 2013, Mrs.Merriam Kiram, descendant of Sulu sultan, came to Dezhou. During her stay, she offered the sacrifices, made a donation and visited the local Sulu descendants, which deepened the bilateral friendship further.

Mr. Bahjin (3rd from the right in the front) Talked with the Descendants From China.

菲律宾苏禄王后裔依百拉吟·巴金（前排右三）与德州苏禄王后裔交谈

将这一具有历史意义的事件铭刻于上。他们在菲律宾期间，阿罗约总统和罗慕洛外长在百忙之中分别接见了他们。阿罗约指出，三位中国苏禄东王后裔重返故土，充分证明中菲友谊不仅仅是三十年，而是源远流长，绵延千年。

2007年7月，菲律宾苏禄王后裔依百拉吟·巴金先生一行到德州祭祖，与居住在德州的苏禄东王后裔亲切交谈，互致问候。苏禄东王后裔还在东王墓前，用伊斯兰教传统的方式进行了祭扫。依百拉吟·巴金先生对中国政府以及德州市为苏禄东王陵墓建设和妥善保护所做的工作表示感谢，希望中菲两国特别是苏禄省与德州市之间的友谊代代相传。

2013年12月，菲律宾苏禄东王后裔梅里安姆·唐劳·基拉姆女士一行九人，赴德州祭拜苏禄王。梅里安姆·唐劳·基拉姆女士一行身着菲律宾传统民族服饰，在阿訇的带领下，庄严地来到东王墓碑前，眼含热泪，诵读经文。诵经结束后，菲律宾客人又缓步绕墓一周，深情的

Mrs. Merriam Tanglao Kiram Offered Sacrifice to Tomb of Paduka Pahala in Dezhou, China.

梅里安姆·唐劳·基拉姆女士一行祭墓

目光扫过墓上一草一木。祭扫活动结束后，梅里安姆·唐劳·基拉姆女士向德州市有关部门赠送了书籍、祈祷手串等礼物，并向苏禄东王墓管理处捐款。而后，菲律宾苏禄东王后裔一行又到苏禄东王墓旁的北营社区走访了德州的苏禄东王后裔，受到了热情的接待。

2017年3月，菲律宾苏禄东王后裔杰赛尔·基拉姆女士在菲律宾总统特使、上好佳集团荣誉董事长施恭旗，菲律宾巴拉望省省长阿尔瓦雷斯，菲律宾华裔青年联合会创会会长洪玉华等的陪同下，来到中国德州，瞻仰苏禄东王墓，纪念先祖来华友好交往六百周年。见到未曾谋面的族人，漂洋过海而来的杰赛尔·基拉姆女士显得尤为激动，她说："中菲两国的友好交往源远流长，苏禄东王墓见证了明代朱棣皇帝与苏禄国王深厚的感情，是两国之间一段令人感动的历史。苏禄王访华六百周年也对菲律宾有重要意义，两国可以重温这段历史，从而在经济、文化、人员等方面的交流上开展更广泛的合作。"

In March 2017, Mrs. Jacel Kiram came to Dezhou to attend the ceremony to mark the 600th Anniversary of Paduka Pahala's visit to China. She expressed that Sulu tomb witnessed the friendship between two countries and this period of history was moving. It was significant for the Philippines to mark the 600th Anniversary of Paduka Pahala's visit to China, by which the people of two countries could go over this period of history to strengthen the bilateral cooperation in economy and culture.

Mrs. Kiram （1st from the right） Presented the Flower Basket to the Tomb of Paduka Pahala

基拉姆女士（右一）向苏禄王墓敬献花篮

In June 2017 when it happened to be 42nd Anniversary of establishment of Sino-Philippine diplomatic relations, An Lizhu (18th generation grandson of Paduka Pahala) and Wen Fang, An Jing (19th generation offsprings) paid a visit to the Philippines at the invitation of Philippine Chinese Federation and Philippine Chinese Traditional Culture Center. On June 9th, they were invited to attend series of activities for celebrating the 42nd anniversary of establishment of Sino-Philippine diplomatic relations and the 600th anniversary of Paduka Pahala's visit to China. On behalf of the descendants in China, An Lizhu gave Philippine Chinese Federation a Chinese handwriting work as a present, and Philippine Chinese Traditional Culture Center presented one in return. In the evening, An Lizhu was invited to watch the theatrical performances. Finally, they promised to inherit the tradition and serve as the goodwill emissary between China and the Philippines.

2017年6月，适逢中菲建交四十二周年之际，德州苏禄东王后裔第十八代孙安立柱，第十九代孙温芳、安静应菲华各界联合会与菲律宾华裔文化传统中心的邀请，访问菲律宾，参加了庆祝菲中建交四十二周年暨纪念苏禄王访华六百年系列活动。6月9日，受邀参加了"超越时空六百年"图片展剪彩仪式，赠送书画作品。安立柱等人向菲律宾菲华各界联合会赠送题为"名昭于史、永世不磨"的中国书法作品，此句取自于明成祖"御制苏禄国东王碑"，高度评价了苏禄王访华的历史功绩。同时还向菲律宾华裔文化传统中心赠送了题为"丝路永畅、友谊长存"的书法作品，寓意今天中华盛世，推行"一带一路"倡议，期盼以此为纽带，发展中菲友好合作。当晚，安立柱一行受邀出席了庆祝菲中建交四十二周年"友谊花盛开"文艺晚会，中菲苏禄东王后裔济济一堂，共话亲情，相约传承先祖传统，共同担当中菲文化交流的友好使者。

An Lizhu（grandson of 18th generation）, Wen Fang, An Jing（offsprings of 19th generation）and Mrs. Jacel Kiram Presented Gifts For Each Other

德州苏禄王后裔第十八代孙安立柱，第十九代孙温芳、安静与菲律宾苏禄东王后裔杰赛尔·基拉姆女士互赠礼品

An Lizhu, Wen Fang and An Jing（Dezhou descendants）Presented the calligraphy works to the Philippine Guests

德州苏禄王后裔第十八代孙安立柱，第十九代孙温芳、安静向菲方赠送书法作品

**The Bridge of Sino-Philippines Friendship**
Marking the 600th Anniversary of the Visit to China by the Sultans of Sulu

奎章
纪念苏禄王访华六百周年

# Sino-Philippine Stakeholders Commemorating Sulu Sultan and Their Cultural Relationship

## 友谊彩桥——中菲人民对苏禄王的缅怀与文化交流

Since the People's Republic of China was founded, especially, since the Philippines built the diplomatic relations with China, the mutual political and cultural exchanges have expanded step by step. At the same time the people of two nations have been holding some activities in memory of Paduka Pahala to pass the friendship on.

In June 1975, Philippine President Ferdinand Marcos with his wife came to visit China, and they were received by Chairman Mao Zedong and Premier Zhou Enlai. In the interview, Marcos mentioned of Paduka Pahala's visit to China 500 years ago. And both hoped to continue the bilateral friendly relations.

苏禄王访华的历史，如今在中国及菲律宾早已传为佳话，成为两国人民的共同骄傲，也为两国人民搭起了一座友谊的彩桥。中菲建交以来，尤其是近年来，两国人民频繁互动交流，共同缅怀苏禄东王。

1975年6月，菲律宾总统菲尔迪南·马科斯和夫人访华，毛泽东主席、周恩来总理亲切会见了马科斯总统一行。在会见中，马科斯总统提到五百多年前苏禄东王访华、客逝于中国的历史。双方共同缅怀了苏禄东王为中菲友好交往所做的贡献，都希望继承中菲人民友好的历史传统，把中菲人民世代和平友好推向前进。

1980年6月，菲律宾驻华大使纳西索·雷耶斯一行四人，专程到山东德州瞻仰苏禄东王墓。苏禄东王墓迎来了

Narciso Reyes, Philippine Ambassador to China（3rd from left）and An Qingshan, Wen Shouling, Grandsons of 16th Generation
菲律宾驻华大使纳西索·雷耶斯先生（左三）与东王后裔第十六代孙安清山、温寿伶

来自东王故土菲律宾的第一批访客。大使一行看到标志着中菲两国人民友谊的苏禄东王墓以及王子墓、王妃墓至今仍保存完好，非常高兴。此后，纳西索·雷耶斯走访了东王后裔，与东王第十六代孙安清山、温寿伶合影留念。纳西索·雷耶斯大使重申：一定珍惜中菲人民的传统友谊，为中菲人民的世代友好做出努力。

1980年7月，中国文化部副部长姚仲明瞻仰苏禄东王墓。中央新闻纪录电影制片厂、人民画报社来到德州，拍摄了苏禄东王墓、清真寺及东王后裔生活、工作状况，重点采访拍摄了时任德州国棉厂厂长的第十八代孙安凤霞。该纪录片成为时任中国文化部部长黄镇访问菲律宾时赠送给马科斯总统的礼物。

1981年12月，以菲律宾原驻华大使、时任东盟秘书长纳西索·雷耶斯为首的文化代表团一行瞻仰苏禄东王墓。中国文化部、山东省文化局、山东省外事部门有关官员及地市领导陪同菲律宾客人，共同缅怀苏禄东王，进一步加深了中菲人民的相互理解，将中菲人民的世代友谊发扬光大。

In June 1980, Philippine ambassador to China Narciso Reyes with other three staff came to pay a respectful visit to Sulu tomb, who were the first guests to Dezhou after 1949. Narciso Reyes had an interview with the descendants of Paduka Pahala and afterwards posed for pictures with An Qingshan and Wen Shouling (16th generation grandson). The ambassador stated that the friendship between China and the Philippines must be cherished and the people of the two countries should make a contribution to it.

In July 1980, a documentary about Sulu tomb, mosque and the life and work status of Sulu descendants was filmed by Central Newsreel and Documentary Film Studio and People Pictorial Society. An Fengxia (18th generation granddaughter) who was the manager of the state-owned textile mill of Dezhou, was interviewed in the film. Later Minister Huang Zhen gave the film to President Ferdinand Marcos as a present.

In December 1981, the Philippine cultural delegation led by ASEAN Secretary General Narciso Reyes , former Philippine ambassador to China came to Dezhou for a visit.

Stage Photo of Chinese Opera: *Sultan and Emperor*
话剧《苏丹与皇帝》剧照

**The Bridge of Sino–Philippines Friendship**
Marking the 600th Anniversary of the Visit to China by the Sultans of Sulu

纪念苏禄王访华六百周年

In 1982, the large-scale stage play Sultan and Emperor produced by Shandong Drama Company caused a sensation. In order to enlarge its effect and make more know about that period of history, a comic book with the same name was published by Shanghai People's Fine Arts Publishing House in 1984. In Octobre. 1986, 36 actors from the Philippines cooperated with Beijing Film Studio to film Sulu Sultan and Chinese Emperor. Some exterior was shot in Dezhou.

苏禄王访华的历史佳话，也引起了中菲文艺界的高度关注。为再现当年苏禄王"航涨海、泛鲸波，不惮数万里之遥"来华访问的艰辛历程及明成祖与苏禄王建立的深厚友谊，1982年，中国山东省话剧团将这段历史编成大型话剧《苏丹与皇帝》，在济南、北京、德州等地上演后，引起强烈反响。为扩大影响，让更多的人了解那段历史，1984年，上海人民美术出版社将《苏丹与皇帝》剧照印成连环画出版发行。1986年10月，菲律宾派出三十六名演员与北京电影制片厂合作，拍摄了故事影片《苏禄国王与中国皇帝》，并在苏禄东王墓现场拍摄外景。中外剧组人员共同瞻仰了苏禄东王墓，缅怀苏禄国王与中国皇帝为奠定中菲传统友谊所做的贡献，一致赞同加强中菲文化交流。

**Stage Photo of Chinese Movie:** *Sulu Sultan and the Chinese Emperor*
《苏禄国王与中国皇帝》电影剧照

1995年3月，菲律宾驻华大使罗穆阿多·翁瞻仰苏禄东王墓。同年12月，罗穆阿多·翁陪同菲律宾苏禄东王后裔依氏麦·基兰先生再次来德州拜谒苏禄东王墓，他在留言簿上写道："永远铭记那段难忘的历史。" 1997年2月，罗穆阿多·翁及夫人随员一行二十多人第三次来到德州瞻仰苏禄东王墓，重申弘扬先辈的传统，继续推动中菲人民的友好关系向前发展。

In March 1995, Philippine ambassador to China Romualdo A. Ong came to look at Sulu tomb with reverence. In December of the same year, the ambassador came again with Mr. Ismail Kiram and he wrote words on the guestbook: Remember the history forever. In February 1997, Mr. Romualdo A. Ong came to Dezhou for the 3rd time and he was warmly welcomed by Dezhou municipal government.

Romualdo A. Ong, Philippine Ambassador to China（2nd from right）Wrote the Inscription
菲律宾驻华大使罗穆阿多·翁先生（右二）为苏禄王墓题词留念

I wish to express deep appreciation and gratitude to the government and people of Shandong Province and Dezhou Municipality for building and maintaining this memorial to the Sultan of Sulu, whose mortal remains lie buried here. He was a guest and good friend of Emperor Zhu Di in the year 1417. This memorial is a lasting monument to Philippines-China Friendship. May this friendship endure forever!

Romualdo A. Ong
Philippine Ambassador to China
12 March 1995

In this, my third visit to Dezhou, I am happy to renew my acquaintance with the city officials and to learn about plans to build a cultural complex around the tomb of the East King of Sulu, whose visit to China in 1417 A.D. was a historic milestone in the centuries-old friendship between the Filipino and Chinese peoples.

Romualdo A. Ong
Philippine Ambassador to China
28 February 1997

## Monument of Sultan Tomb Made By China and the Philippines
苏禄王墓纪念碑

On May 17th, 2000, President Joseph Estrada visited China and attended the banquet in memory of the 25th anniversary of the diplomatic relations between China and the Philippines. He addressed that it was worth mentioning that the monument of Sulu Sultan in Dezhou city was preserved well as the symbol of friendship between two nations, which we were all proud of.

In March 2005, Alberto G. Romulo, Minister of Foreign Affairs of Republic of the Philippines, came to Asia Pacific Research Institute of Chinese Academy of Social Sciences, where he delivered an address that the friendship between China and the Philippines had a long history and showed a new look. In his speech, he not only looked back on the history but also made positive comment on the good progress of the bilateral relations since the two countries established diplomatic relations 30 years ago.

In April 2005, President Hu Jintao paid a state visit to the Philippines at the invitation who made an important speech at the joint meeting of the Senate and the House of Representatives. Presi-

1999 年 8 月，菲律宾驻华大使罗穆阿多·翁与德州市市长举行苏禄东王墓纪念碑揭幕仪式。此碑系菲律宾社团与菲律宾苏禄东王后裔联合铸造的铁质英文碑，与中文碑并列镶嵌在基座上，象征着中菲友谊丰碑永续。

2000 年 5 月，菲律宾总统约瑟夫·埃斯特拉达访华。17 日，埃斯特拉达总统在出席庆祝中菲建交二十五周年宴会上的致辞中说："特别值得一提的是，在山东省德州市，作为菲中两国人民友谊象征的苏禄王纪念碑仍被保存下来。今天，我们为能继续加强这一源远流长的友好交往而感到自豪。"

2005 年 3 月，菲律宾外交部部长阿尔贝尔多·罗慕洛来到中国社会科学院亚洲太平洋研究所，发表了题为"菲中关系——古老的友谊，崭新的气象"的演讲。罗慕洛在演讲中回顾了菲中两国源远流长的友好往来，追溯明朝永乐年间中菲两国人民的友谊，缅怀了苏禄东王访华和中菲两国人民友好往来的历史渊源。他高度评价两国建交三十年来双边关系的发展。

2005 年 4 月，中国国家主席胡锦涛应邀对菲律宾共和国进行国事访问。他在菲律宾国会参众两院联席会议上发表重要演讲，指出："中国和菲律宾一水相隔、比邻而居，两国人民的传统友谊源远流长。五百多年前，苏禄国王带着菲律宾人民的美好愿望踏上前往中国的友谊之路，在中菲友好史上留下了脍炙人口的佳话。"

2005 年 5 月，菲律宾驻华大使盖威利携使馆官员、工作人员以及三十多名在华工作的菲律宾社团成员，乘专车到德州瞻仰苏禄东王墓。

2007 年 7 月，菲律宾苏禄省副省长安娜·沙依都利亚女士率领菲律宾苏禄访华团，专程到德州拜谒苏禄东王墓。

2014 年 1 月，上好佳集团（中国）有限公司董事长、菲律宾籍华人施恭旗先生，菲律宾华裔青年联合会会长洪玉华女士率代表团一行拜谒苏禄东王墓。两年来，施恭旗

dent Hu Jintao pointed out that China and the Philippines are neighbors and the friendship between two nations dated back long. The mutual business activities began one thousand years ago. And five hundred years ago, Sulu Sultan came to China with the blessing of the Philippine people, which was praised wide and far in the history.

In May 2005, the Philippine ambassador to China Willy C. Gaa along with his staff and 30 members of the Philippine associations in China came to Dezhou to pay a respectful visit to Sulu tomb, who were received warmly by the local government.

In July 2005, a Philippine delegation led by the vice governor of Sulu Province Anna Shahriyah came to Dezhou.

In January 2014, Shi Gongqi, chairman of Shanghaojia Group（China）, a Filipino Chinese and Hong Yuhua, President of Philippines Chinese Youth Federation came to visit the monument of Sulu Sultan. In the past two years, Shi Gongqi had been to Dezhou for

Mr. Shi Gongqi and Mrs. Hong Yuhua Visited the Tomb of Paduka Pahala

施恭旗先生、洪玉华女士一行拜谒苏禄王墓

Anna, Vice Governor of Sulu Province（5th from right）Looked Up At the Tomb of Paduka Pahala.

苏禄省副省长安娜·沙依都利亚（右五）瞻仰苏禄东王墓

five times and made a donation of more than 3,000,000 RMB as maintenance funds. And Hong Yuhua as an envoy of friendship came to Dezhou for 6 times and helped the descendants of two nations to bring about the mutual visits.

In November 2014, a Philippine Art Troupe came to Dezhou, accompanied by Mr. Shi Gongqi, the Philippine Ambassador to China and the Mayor of Laganyan City, and their wonderful performances gave the local people a deep impression, which promoted the art and culture relation between two nations further.

On October 20th, 2016, Philippine President Rodrigo Duterte visited China at the invitation and was interviewed by President Xi Jinping, who put forward four proposals on the future of Sino-Philippine relations and suggested that some memorial activities of the 600th anniversary of Sulu Sultan's visiting to China should be held next year.

The Laganyan Art Trope hold a grand cultural exchange performance between Philippines and China in Dezhou

拉甘岩艺术团前来德州开展菲中文艺交流演出

先生先后五次拜谒苏禄东王墓，向苏禄东王墓捐赠修缮基金三百余万元人民币。洪玉华女士先后六次拜谒苏禄东王墓，多次促成并资助菲律宾苏禄东王后裔与德州苏禄东王后裔认宗互访，成为中菲友好的使者。

2014 年 11 月，上好佳集团董事长施恭旗先生及菲律宾驻华大使、菲律宾拉甘岩市市长率领拉甘岩艺术团前来德州拜谒苏禄国东王墓，并为德州人民奉献了一场精彩演出，促进了两国文化艺术交流。

2016 年 10 月，菲律宾总统杜特尔特应邀访华。20 日，中国国家主席习近平同杜特尔特总统进行会谈，就中菲关系的未来发展提出四点建议，其中第三点是双方要推动民间往来。习近平主席指出，中方建议两国就 2017 年菲律宾苏禄王首次赴华六百周年开展系列纪念活动。

2017 年 5 月，为纪念苏禄王访华六百周年，北京市侨联、菲律宾归侨联谊会、北京大学等单位共同举办了"中国与菲律宾古苏禄国友好交往历史研讨会——纪念苏禄王访华六百周年"。5 月 14 日，与会人员由北京市侨联、菲律宾归侨联谊会会长庄移山先生带队来到德州拜谒苏禄东王墓，并与德州苏禄文化博物馆、德州北营苏禄东王后裔代表举行系列纪念活动。

2017 年 9 月 13 日，德州苏禄王后裔联谊会、菲律宾归侨联谊会、菲律宾苏禄东王后裔等共同举办了"纪念苏禄王访华六百周年"盛典。来自全国的苏禄王后裔代表（包括德州北营根脉及北京、天津、河北、辽宁等二十五个支脉）四百余人、菲律宾苏禄王后裔（包括普戈达尔·基拉姆先生、纳瓦尔·坦女士、巴塔鲁丁·基拉姆先生、杰赛尔·基拉姆女士等 30 余人）及菲律宾归侨联谊会、菲律宾华裔

In May 2017, a seminar on the Friendly Relationship between China and Ancient Sulu was held by Federation of Returned Overseas Chinese of Beijing City, Federation of Returned Overseas Chinese form Philippines and Beijing University in memory of the 600th anniversary of Sulu Sultan's visit to China. On May 14th, all the attendances led by Mr. Zhuang Yishan came to visit Sulu tomb and meanwhile held some memorial activities with Sulu Culture Museum and the local descendants of Paduka Pahala.

On September 13th, 2017, a grand ceremony for marking the 600th anniversary of Sulu Sultan's visit to China was held by Federation of Sulu Descendants of Dezhou City, Federation of Returned Overseas Chinese form Philippines and Philippine Sulu Sultan's offspring. More than 500 guests were present. The ceremony was co-hosted by Mrs. Jacel Kiram, with the presence of Mr. Phugdalon Kiram and An Lizhu （the 18th generation grandson of Paduka Pahala）. At the ceremony, the imam read the Koran and Mr.phugdaion Kiram

Mr.An Lizhu gave philippine guests *The Genealogy of Wen-An Family* as gift
族长安立柱向苏丹、公主赠送《温安通谱》

made a speech. Afterwards, some guests and descendants delivered the addresses in memory of Paduka Pahala's great historical deed in succession. Finally, on behalf of the Sulu descendants in China, An Lizhu gave Pedigree of An-Wen Clan of Sulu Descendants in China, the disk and the family badge to Sulu Mr. Phugdalon Kiram as a present, and Mrs. Jacel Kiram presented him a royal robe in return. The ceremony was reported in front page by the Xinhua News Agency and other news medias and web sites, which has caused the great social sensation.

青年联合会、菲中关系发展促进会（香港）等嘉宾共五百余人济济一堂，参加了盛典。德州苏禄王后裔第十八代孙安立柱先生与菲律宾苏禄王后裔普戈达尔·基拉姆先生共同主持庄严的祭墓仪式，阿訇诵读《古兰经》，基拉姆先生致祭辞，誓言：继承先祖遗训，将中菲友谊世世代代延续下去。来自中菲两国的嘉宾及全国苏禄王后裔代表分别致辞，缅怀苏禄东王的历史功绩，铭记历史，谨守祖训，为两国人民搭起一道友好交往的彩桥。最后，安立柱先生代表中国苏禄王后裔向基拉姆先生赠送《中华苏禄东王后裔——温安通谱》、特制纪念盘及家族族徽等，杰赛尔·基拉姆女士回赠王袍一套。回族书法家康书贵先生当场挥毫泼墨，写下题为"传承历史、继往开来"系列书法作品赠予基拉姆先生，表达了中菲人民的共同心愿。这次盛典，引起了很大的社会反响，新华社国际头条进行了报导，各大新闻媒体及网站纷纷转载。

中菲苏禄东王后裔合影

　　六百年前运河上船队的浩浩荡荡和当年苏禄国使团的艰辛与荣耀，都已经随着历史远去。古老的苏禄东王墓依旧庄严肃穆，粼粼的运河水依旧在不远处荡漾着，他们似乎在用六百年的时光证明：海上丝绸之路，从来都不只是物资往来与商品贸易的载体，它为探索与相逢创造了可能，而相遇、相识、相知，又为它催发出新的动力，让人策马前行，扬帆海上。

　　正如习近平主席所说："这些开拓事业之所以名垂青史，是因为使用的不是战马和长矛，而是驼队和善意；依靠的不是坚船和利炮，而是宝船和友谊。"当一个个繁忙港口中的大船鸣笛起航时，浪花之上，托起的将是中国作为负责任大国与域内外国家的深厚友谊，是"21 世纪海上丝绸之路"沿线国家对繁荣与和平的共同期许。

The mighty fleets on the Grand Canal 600 years ago and the hardship and glory of the Sulu diplomatic corps have gone with the history. The ancient Sulu Tomb looks still solemn and respectful as before and not far away from here the water of the Grand Canal is still shimmering, all of which seem to prove that for 600 years the Maritime Silk Road has never been only a carrier of goods exchanges. As a matter of fact, it has been creating the possibilities for exploration and encounter, and now it is bringing the new vitality to the friendly communication between two countries.

As Chairman of China, Xi Jinping said, "the reason why these pioneering undertakings are crowned with eternal glory is that they do not depended on battle horses and spears, but camels and goodwill, on the vessels with treasure and friendship rather than the battleships and the artillery". A huge vessel will set off from the bustling port with the goodwill of China, a responsible power, which is the common expectation for prosperity and peace all the countries along the 21st Maritime Silk Road possess.

# *Postscript*

600 years ago, Emperor Yongle of Ming Dynasty and the Sultans of Sulu developed a friendship between China and the Philippines in Beijing. Nowadays, Chairman Xi Jinping also have thought about how to be strategic for the future of Sino-Philippine relations with President Duterte in Beijing. The book titled *The Bridge of Sino-Philippine Friendship, Marking the 600th Anniversary of the Visit to China by the Sultans of Sulu*, is a symbol of the friendly relations between the two countries.

After the Chinese version of the book was published, it has aroused great repercussions in the society. Based on the first edition, this revision added English content to further expand the propaganda value.

Thanks for the strong support from the government; Thank the author, Professor Wang Shoudong, for his vigorous spirits of scholarly research; Thank Professor Hu Yanfeng for translating this book; Thank Professor Zhu Yafei, Professor Zhao Shuguo and Professor Zheng Weikuan for their comments.

Thank Mr. Yang Shengjiang and Mr. Wu Qingzun for their helps.

Special thanks to Mr. Romana, the Ambassador of the Philippines to China, and Mrs. Killam for writing preface to this book.

July 2018

# 出版后记

　　奎章，其本义古指帝王的诗文书法，今泛指杰出的文章。600 年前，中国明朝永乐皇帝在北京与苏禄王为中国与菲律宾的友谊开篇创史；600 年后，习近平主席同样也是在北京与杜特尔特总统为中菲关系的未来谋篇布局。本书取名"奎章"，其寓意正是两国元首共同书写中菲关系宏伟篇章的写照。

　　2017 年 9 月，本书第一版付梓，在社会上引起较大反响。本次改版，是为适应文化交流的需要，在第一版的基础上新增英文内容，以进一步拓展原书的宣传价值。

　　本书从策划到出版，得到政府部门的高度重视和大力支持。本书作者王守栋教授几易其稿，其严谨的治学精神、精益求精的态度，令我们感到钦佩。德州学院胡延峰教授所学虽为英语专业，但对本书历史文献的翻译，可令读者深刻感受到其深厚的专业素养与功底。山东师范大学历史学专家朱亚非教授、赵树国教授，以及广西民族大学历史学专家郑维宽教授，对本书提出了无私的意见和宝贵的建议，让本书的学术更加严谨，史学价值更加丰盈。在此，我们一并致以衷心的感谢！

　　同时亦要感谢中菲苏禄王后裔联合会会长杨胜江先生、北京市侨联菲律宾归侨联谊会常务理事吴卿樽先生为推动本书赴菲开展文化交流所提供的帮助！

　　特别感谢菲律宾驻华大使罗马纳先生、菲律宾苏禄王后裔基拉姆女士为本书作序！

2018 年 7 月

**图书在版编目（CIP）数据**

奎章：纪念苏禄王访华六百周年 / 王守栋著；
胡延峰译—2版. —桂林：广西师范大学出版社，
2018.7

ISBN 978-7-5598-0115-9

Ⅰ.①奎… Ⅱ.①王…②胡… Ⅲ.①中外关系—国
际关系史—史料—菲律宾 Ⅳ.①D829.341

中国版本图书馆CIP数据核字（2017）第318586号

总 策 划　张艺兵

策划编辑　黄　毓　张昀珠

责任编辑　张昀珠　黄　毓　黄佳梦　韦兰琴　黄玉东

责任校对　黄丽江　葛　夏

英文校对　杨昕然

整体设计　刘　凛　梁雪芬　黄小纯

线描插画　苏冬生

广西师范大学出版社出版发行

（广西桂林市五里店路9号　邮政编码：541004）

网址：http://www.bbtpress.com

出版人：张艺兵

服务电话：0771-2092860

全国新华书店经销

广西民族印刷包装集团有限公司印刷

（广西南宁市高新区高新三路1号　邮政编码：530007）

开本：787 mm × 1 092 mm　　　1/12

印张：$11\frac{8}{12}$　　字数：150 千字

2018 年 7 月第 2 版　　　2018 年 7 月第 1 次印刷

定价：188.00 元